SYSTEMS DESIGN AND DOCUMENTATION

COMPUTER SCIENCE SERIES

COMPUTER SCIENCE SERIES

SYSTEMS DESIGN AND DOCUMENTATION

An Introduction to the HIPO Method

Harry Katzan, Jr.
Chairman, Computer Science Department
Pratt Institute

VNR VAN NOSTRAND REINHOLD COMPANY
NEW YORK   CINCINNATI   ATLANTA   DALLAS   SAN FRANCISCO
LONDON   TORONTO   MELBOURNE

Van Nostrand Reinhold Company Regional Offices:
New York Cincinnati Atlanta Dallas San Francisco

Van Nostrand Reinhold Company International Offices:
London Toronto Melbourne

Library of Congress Catalog Card Number: 76-9785
ISBN: 0-442-24267-0

Manufactured in the United States of America

Published by Van Nostrand Reinhold Company
450 West 33rd Street, New York, N.Y. 10001

Published simultaneously in Canada by Van Nostrand Reinhold Ltd.

15 14 13 12 11 10 9 8 7 6 5 4 3 2

Library of Congress Cataloging in Publication Data

Katzan, Harry.
  Systems design and documentation.

  (Computer science series)
  Includes bibliographies and index.
  1. HIPO technique.   2. System analysis.
I. Title.
QA402. K329   003   76-9785
ISBN 0-442-24267-0

PREFACE

One of the realities of modern life is that we all exist in a world of systems—or more precisely, in a system of systems. Economic, social, and governmental systems are obvious examples of systems to which we are accustomed. There are others. We may, for example, use a logical or philosophical system to render an explanation for a phenomenon and use a mathematical or statistical system to develop a prediction for the occurrence of a possible event. In modern technology, common examples of systems are a transportation system, a data processing system, and a security system. Because most systems are complex and because we frequently are part of the system under study, we customarily employ models of systems for planning, analysis, and decision making. In general, models of systems can range from mathematical equations to physical replicas and serve to describe a system for purposes of explanation, analysis, prediction, or development. The quality of a model is a function of how closely it approximates the real system for the purposes at hand.

A large class of natural, human, and technological systems are input and output oriented. Systems of this type interact with their environment by accepting input and producing output as a part of their normal functioning. Computer and information systems are well-known examples of input and output oriented systems; however, almost any organization that interacts with people and produces a tangible result would serve as an equally good example. Most existing techniques for modeling input and output oriented systems describe the structure of the system and relegate the set of inputs, the set of outputs, and the functions performed by the system to a secondary role in the description. Thus, existing techniques, such as flow diagrams, decision tables, and verbal descriptions, do not support the processes of planning, analysis, and decision making mentioned above.

The purpose of this book is to introduce a new technique for describing input and output oriented systems. The new technique, known as HIPO—which stands for *Hierarchy, plus Input, Process, Output*—is used to describe a system in terms of its inputs, outputs, and constituent processes, and places these functions in a meaningful hierarchy. The significance of the HIPO concept lies in the fact that it is used to describe *what a system does*, instead of how it does it, and is thereby useful for planning, analysis, and decision making. HIPO can be used for system design, system development, system analysis, and system documentation.

The HIPO method was developed in the data processing field for describing systems and programs. However, it is generally felt that the concepts have wider applicability and would be useful for describing other classes of systems as well. As a result, the book supports the more comprehensive audience by including a brief introduction to systems concepts in addition to a presentation of the HIPO technique.

HIPO can be classed as a documentation technique because it is used for describing systems and programs. However, this is a narrow view of its applicability. The methodology achieves its greatest utility when it is used as a design aid, as a development tool, and finally as a documentation technique. When HIPO is used in this manner, documentation becomes a natural by-product of design and development and the events in the system life cycle can be placed in proper perspective.

It is a pleasure to acknowledge the cooperation of the IBM Corporation in granting permission to include IBM copyrighted material and the assistance of my wife Margaret in the preparation of the manuscript.

HARRY KATZAN, JR.

CONTENTS

SYSTEMS DESIGN AND DOCUMENTATION

1 | INTRODUCTION TO SYSTEMS THINKING

INTRODUCTION

The primary objective of this book is to introduce a new system design and documentation technique known as HIPO. The acronym HIPO stands for Hierarchy *plus* Input-Process-Output, and the methodology provides a graphical description of the functions performed by a system and the relationship between the inputs, the processes, and the outputs of that system. Because the functions of a system are described and not its organization and logic, a HIPO description provides information on "what a system does," and is thereby useful at most stages of planning, development, and implementation. A HIPO description is particularly useful from the management point of view since it allows decisions to be based on the function of a system rather than on structure and implementation, which tend to obscure the reasons for having the system in the first place.

The HIPO technique can be used to describe any system at all levels of complexity, and for example, would be just as useful for describing the processes of government as it is for showing the function of a computer-oriented system or program. The description of a system using the HIPO concept is called a *HIPO package;* it consists of a hierarchy diagram showing the functions of the system at vary-

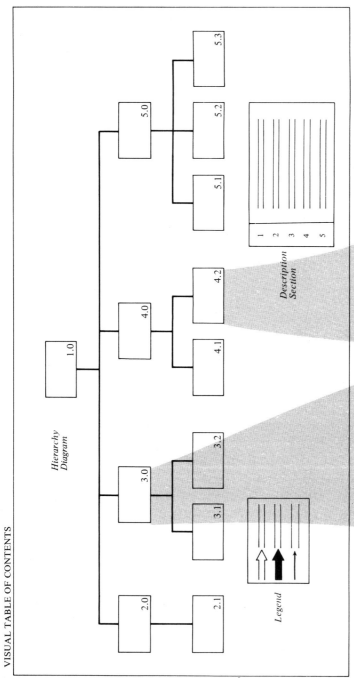

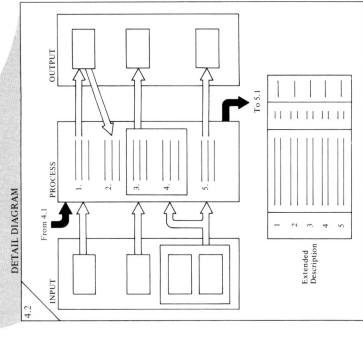

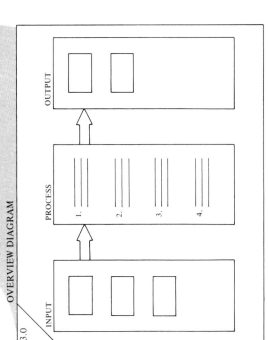

Figure 1.1   General form of a HIPO package.

ing levels of detail and input-process-output diagrams for each element in the structure. Figure 1.1 depicts the general form of a HIPO package. It is important, however, to place the process of describing and documenting systems in perspective. While the HIPO method must ultimately take its place alongside other systems techniques, it represents a new order—a change to the well-established methodology of decision tables, flow diagrams, and lengthy descriptions. The situation is summarized well by Machiavelli in *The Prince.**

> . . . there is nothing more difficult to take in hand, more perilous to conduct, or more uncertain in its success, than to take the lead in the introduction of a new order of things. Because the innovator has for enemies all those who have done well under the old conditions, and lukewarm defenders in those who may do well under the new. This coolness arises partly from fear of the opponents, who have the laws on their side, and partly from the incredulity of men, who do not readily believe in new things until they have a long experience of them.

SYSTEMS PERSPECTIVES

The design, description, and analysis of systems is not an outgrowth of the computer revolution, even though there has been a noticeable increase in systems-related activity in recent years rising out of the widespread use of computers. In fact, ancient philosophers were concerned with "systems of society" in early Egyptian and Greek cultures, and that concern is reflected in the modern interest in systems science that now pervades the areas of mathematics, systems engineering, cybernetics, philosophy, behavioral sciences, computer science, biology, and certain parts of physics. The study of systems-related concepts has considerable relevance for the modern man. Listen to Ludwig von Bertalanffy:†

> Modern science is characterized by its ever-increasing specialization, necessitated by the enormous amount of data, the complexity of techniques and of theoretical structures within every field. Thus science is split into innumerable disciplines continually generating new subdisciplines. In consequence, the physicist, the biologist, the psychologist and the social scientist are, so to speak, encapsulated in their private universes, and it is difficult to get word from one cocoon to the other.
>
> This, however, is opposed by another remarkable aspect. Surveying the

*Machiavelli, p. 9.
†von Bertalanffy, p. 30.

evolution of modern science, we encounter a surprising phenomenon. Independently of each other, similar problems and conceptions have evolved in widely different fields.

The phenomenon that Bertalanffy mentions is widely recognized and there is no scarcity of publications in a variety of forms on systems-related topics. In fact, several versions of a taxonomy of systems are in existence and methods of classification are reasonably well known. For example, Beer* suggests an arbitrary classification of systems based on two distinct criteria: complexity and the attribute of being deterministic or probabilistic. *Complexity* refers to the number of relations or connections among components of the system and *deterministic/probabilistic* refers to the extent to which the interactions between components can be predicted. The two criteria permit the following classification of systems to be established:

1. *Simple deterministic*—a system with few components and interactions, such as the game of billiards.
2. *Complex deterministic*—a complicated system that responds to input conditions in a perfectly predicatable way, such as the electronic computer.
3. *Simple probabilistic*—a system with few components whose behavior cannot be predicted, such as a statistical quality control system.
4. *Complex probabilistic*—a complicated system, such as the economy, or a living process, whose behavior cannot be predicted in advance.†

Clearly, Beer's classification is one of many that have been developed.

In an analogous technique to that of classification, a collection of general methods has surfaced for describing systems. Van Court Hare‡ surveys methods of defining systems that include graph-theoretic methods, flow diagrams, networks, input/output analysis, and matrix methods. To be sure, these are effective techniques for analysis, diagnosis, and optimization. But what about system design evaluation, and subsequently documentation? One reasonably well-known approach to the latter activity is called the "systems approach."

*Beer, *Cybernetics and Management*, pp. 12-19.
†Actually, Beer classifies the economy as being an "exceedingly complex probabilistic" system; however, the point has been made and a more detailed classification is not needed.
‡Hare, pp. 13-24.

THE SYSTEMS APPROACH

The systems approach is a way of thinking about a system that centers around the objectives of the system. The approach is commensurate with the basic concept of a system, which is defined as a set of components that work together toward an overall objective. The systems approach places a heavy emphasis on a description of the functions of the system, or stated in another manner, a description of what we are planning to do.

Churchman* gives a good example of the systems approach to automotive transportation:

> For example, if I ask you to describe an automobile, you may immediately switch off your thinking process and simply blurt out the things you recall about your own automobile—its wheels, engine, and shape. You start by saying, "Well, an automobile is something that has four wheels and is driven by an engine." I (in an attempt to switch on your thinking process) ask whether a three-wheeled automobile is a possibility. You have seen one and will readily admit this change in your description, still without thinking much about the meaning of the change. I, becoming more belligerent, pursue the matter further and ask you whether a two-wheeled automobile is a possibility. You begin to look puzzled, thus indicating that your thinking has been turned on at a low voltage. I go on, being cheerfully disagreeable, and ask you whether an automobile without any wheels whatsoever is also a possibility. You become more puzzled and think not about automobiles but about silly question posers. Yet to consider the wheel-less automobile is a creative way of looking at this system we call the automobile. It may be that the need for wheels is one of the major producers of traffic congestion and the inconvenience of the current automobile. An automobile that can float a few feet off the surface of the earth might provide a far more comfortable ride and produce far fewer problems of traffic congestion and even of accidents. And floating automobiles may be technically feasible in the future.
>
> The way to describe an automobile is *first* by thinking about what it is for, about its *function,* and not the list of items that make up its structure. If you begin by thinking about the function of the automobile, that is, what it is for, then you won't describe the automobile by talking about its four wheels, its engine, size, and so on. You will begin by thinking that an automobile is a mechanical means of transporting a few people from one place to another, at a certain prescribed cost. As soon as you begin to think in this manner, then your "description" of the automobile begins to take on new and often quite radical aspects. That's the systems approach to automotive transportation.

*Churchman, pp. 12–13.

Systems design and analysis is a form of planning and most planners in organizations are familiar with a common problem. Summarized briefly, the problem is that planners must synthesize a complete plan before managers react, and it is commonplace to see the whole plan rejected. The reason is actually quite simple. Planners and decision makers normally operate at different conceptual levels. The planner is concerned with structural and operative details, while the manager is concerned with social/political/economic factors. To each group, the other's activity is considered to be "less necessary."

The systems approach to planning, therefore, emphasizes activity such as "teaching the plan" so as to create a working relationship between the planner and the decision maker. Clearly, a decision maker may not be in a position to evaluate structure and operation, but he can evaluate function. This is the essence of the systems approach, which is measured by the degree to which it can promote understanding and acceptance.

HIERARCHY AND FUNCTION

Essentially, what we plan to do is to describe a system by abstracting from it only the proportion of interest in the design and decision-making processes—namely its function. The technique simplifies the analysis by reducing the concern over the internal structure of the system. The approach is well established in scientific methodology and is well summarized by Herbert A. Simon:*

> We are seldom interested in explaining or predicting phenomena in all their particularity; we are usually interested only in a few properties abstracted from the complex reality.

The technique of modeling only those aspects of a system that are necessary to an ongoing task in inherent in the top-down strategy of scientific development. This hierarchical "attack" is further explained by Simon:†

> We knew a great deal about the gross physical and chemical behavior of matter before we had a knowledge of molecules, a great deal about molecules, a great deal about molecular chemistry before we had an atomic theory, and a great deal about atoms before we had any theory of ele-

*Simon, p. 16.
†*Ibid.*, p. 17.

mentary particles. . . This skyhook-skyscraper construction of science from the roof down to the yet unconstructed foundations was possible because the behavior of the system at each level depended on only a very approximate, simplified, abstracted characterization of the system at the level next beneath.

The use of hierarchy as a component of a descriptive methodology is a means of reducing complexity and is particularly useful when the concern centers around the function of a system that results primarily from the organization of components, and is relatively independent of the structural properties of the individual components.

INPUT AND OUTPUT

Most systems accept input and produce output. Input can take one of the following forms: the setting of a switch or level, the setting of a parameter, or data recorded on an input medium of some kind. Similarly, output can take the form of an output signal, the positioning of a dial or meter, or data recorded or displayed on an output medium. When the input/output relationship of a system is sufficiently stable so that reliable predictions can be made of the system's behavior, then the system can be referred to as a "black box" system and the operations performed by the system are regarded as a transformation. An input/output system of this type, also known as a *transducer,* is defined optionally by describing what transformation takes place but not how that transformation is implemented.

The relationship between the hierarchical structure of a system and its input/output characteristics is demonstrated in Figure 1.2. The description of the inputs and the outputs at each hierarchical level is complete; at lower levels in the hierarchy, the specification of the transformation between inputs and outputs is more detailed than at higher levels, and the outputs of one phase in the process may serve as inputs to a subsequent phase of the same process.

COMMUNICATION

Coordination between components of a system is achieved through methods of communication, which can take the form of control signals or data. In fact, communication is the ingredient that ties a system together. The notion of a system is not restricted to machines and related artifacts, but also includes natural and human systems. When human systems are involved, "communication is a

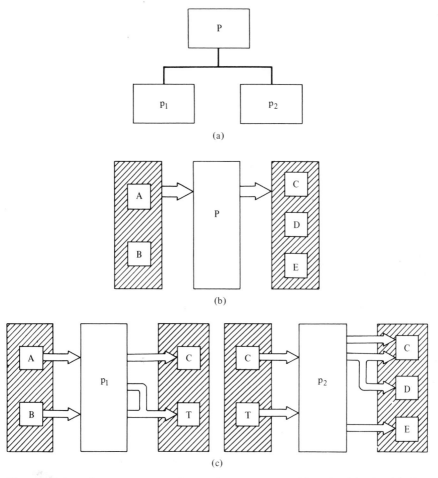

Figure 1.2 Input/output structure of a sample system at two hierarchical levels. (a) Hierarchical structure; (b) input/output structure at first level; (c) input/output structure at second level.

social affair"* and the method of communication normally takes the form of language. However, human communication is not entirely restricted to language, in the usual sense, and language is enhanced, so to speak, by habits of gesture, social conventions and formalities, and rules of membership—to name only a few. Cherry† has the following to say about communication in modern society:

*Cherry, p. 3.
†*Ibid.*, p. 5.

But life in the modern world is coming to depend more and more upon "technical" means of communication, telephone, and telegraph, radio and printing. Without such technical aids the modern city-state could not exist one week, for it is only be means of them that trade and business can proceed; that goods and services can be distributed where needed; that railways can run on a schedule; that law and order are maintained; that education is possible. Communication renders true social life practicable, for communication means organization. Communications have enabled the social unit to grow, from the village to the town, to the modern city-state, until today we see organized systems of mutual dependence grown to cover whole hemispheres.

The technical means of communication permits modern organizations to exist and allows managers and administrators to exercise their responsibilities. Management operates through a model of the business* and customarily uses a subjective institutional language for discussing the facts and models of reality.

Organizations are systems and effective methods for designing and describing systems can be used for documenting the functions of the organization as well as for designing and documenting systems that exist as components in the system. In the parlay of modern management, descriptive techniques are an effective decision-making tool.

DESCRIPTION AND DOCUMENTATION

In the development of systems, several types of activities are normally included that exist independently of the specific system being developed. The activities are classed as follows:†

1. Initial design.
2. Concept evaluation.
3. Detail functional design.
4. Implementation and testing.
5. Documentation and system support.
6. Education, maintenance, and system modification.

These activities are summarized in Figure 1.3.

The requirements for systems description at the various stages of development are provided through the various components of a HIPO package. Because a HIPO package is visual and describes function and not structure, effective decisions regarding systems activity

---

*Beer, *Decision and Control*, p. 123.

†An example of these activities applied to the program development process is given in *Improved Programming Technology*, pp. 2.14–2.16.

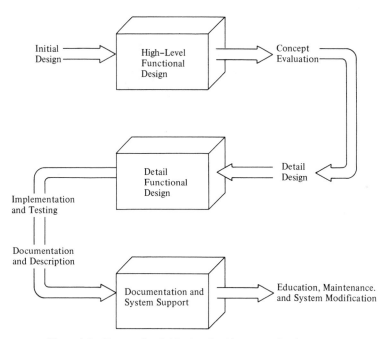

Figure 1.3 Classes of activities involved in system development.

can be made before the system is actually synthesized and the point of no return is passed.   The relationship of the systems developed effort to the total system life cycle is covered in subsequent chapters.

REFERENCES

Beer, S., *Cybernetics and Management*, New York, John Wiley & Sons, Inc., 1959.

Beer, S., *Decision and Control,* New York, John Wiley and Sons, Inc., 1966.

Cherry, C., *On Human Communication: A Review, A Survey, and A Criticism* (2nd Edition), Cambridge, Mass., The M.I.T. Press, 1966.

Churchman, C. W., *The Systems Approach*, New York, Dell Publishing Company, 1968.

Hare, Jr., V. C., *Systems Analysis: A Diagnostic Approach*, New York, Harcourt, Brace and World, Inc., 1967.

Improved Programming Technology, White Plains, N.Y., IBM Corporation, Form SH20-1498, 1974.

Machiavelli, N., *The Prince* (1513), Translated by W. K. Marriott and published in *Great Books of the Western World,* Volume 23, Chicago, Encyclopaedia Britannica, Inc., 1952.

Simon, H. A., *The Sciences of the Artificial,* Cambridge, Mass., The M.I.T. Press, 1969.

von Bertalanffy, L., *General System Theory*, New York, George Braziller, 1968.

2 | A TAXONOMY OF SYSTEMS CONCEPTS

INTRODUCTION

The application of systems thinking is relevant to a large class of problems ranging from computer programs prepared by an individual to the study of large organizations. Moreover, systems thinking encompasses phenomena regardless of their origin or complexity. Thus, the systems approach is just as appropriate for the study of a biological organism as it is for the analysis of a computer system. Systems thinking must be carried out systematically to be a useful approach to problems involving systems, and therefore, should be based on a solid foundation of systems concepts.

One of the difficulties that is frequently encountered in the study of systems is that concepts and terminology are not standardized. Different terms are used to refer to the same concept and the same term is used to refer to different concepts. The objective of this chapter, therefore, is to present a conceptual framework that can be used as a starting place for the understanding of the large amount of diverse literature on the subject. Not every concept given here is used in other chapters, but the conceptual framework as a whole is necessary for effective systems thinking.

The taxonomy of systems concepts given here is a summarization and a discussion of a set of definitions in a "system of systems concepts" developed by Ackoff.* Ackoff's basic definitions are enclosed in quotation marks.

SYSTEMS CONCEPTS

The notion of exactly what constitutes a system is subjective in the sense that the boundaries and characteristics of a particular system are determined by the objectives of the observer. The following definitions outline the basic considerations:

1. "A *system* is a set of interrelated elements."
2. "An *abstract system* is one all of whose elements are concepts."
3. "A *concrete system* is one at least two of whose elements are objects."
4. "The *state of a system* at a moment of time is the set of relevant properties which that system has at that time."
5. "The *environment of a system* is a set of elements and their relevant properties, which elements are not part of the system but a change in any of which can produce a change in the state of the system."

In a system, therefore, every element must be related in some manner with at least one other element of that system. The relationships connect the elements of the system together, so they can be regarded as a single entity, and can take the form of a physical connection, a logical similarity, a causal rule, and so forth. Systems exist with the support of an environment, and in many cases, the environment determines the nature of the system itself. The abstract system of mathematics, for example, exists within the system of formal logic. The system of formal logic is the environment of the system of mathematics.

The subjectivity of systems concepts is related to the observer. To the computer engineer, for example, a computer processing unit is a system of gates and interconnections. To the computer systems architect, on the other hand, the processing unit is an element in the total computer system that consists of the processing unit, the main storage unit, peripheral devices, and other equipment. The computer system is the environment of the processing unit; other elements that

*Ackoff, pp. 661–671.

exist in the environment of the processing unit are the computer software and the application programs. Software and application programs, along with data, are the environment of the computer system. Similarly, the data processing system is a part of a larger organization, such as a business, and the larger organization is an element in a still larger system, such as a political or economic system. Thus, every system can be viewed conceptually as being an element of a larger system.

A concrete system exists in real life in the sense that, for example, you can "paint it red." The objects that constitute a concrete system possess attributes that determine the characteristics of the system at any point in time; this is the state of the system. The state of a political body at a given point in time regarding a particular piece of legislative action is determined collectively by the voting preference of the constituent members.

TYPES OF SYSTEMS

Systems are classified according to our conceptualization of them. We may choose to consider some properties and ignore others depending upon the purpose of our classification. The following definitions are relevant to systems classification:

1. "A *closed system* is one that has no environment. An *open system* is one that does."
2. "A system (or environmental) *event* is a change in one or more structural properties of the system (or its environment) over a period of time of specified duration, that is, a change in the structural state of the system (or environment)."
3. "A *static (one-state) system* is one to which no events happen."
4. "A *dynamic (multi-state) system* is one to which events happen, whose state changes over time."
5. "A *homeostatic system* is a static system whose elements and environment are dynamic."

A closed system is self-contained and has no interaction with an environment; an example of this type of system would be a closed ecological system of the type that was once envisioned for use on space vehicles. (A closed system is distinct from a closed feedback cycle that does not require human input; for example, an autopilot is a system with a closed feedback cycle whereas an automobile system is a system with an open feedback cycle because of the participation of the driver.)

An event that changes the state of a system under consideration or its environment is of interest to the systems scientist. Clearly, any occurrence in the real or abstract world is an event to some system, and that occurrence can originate from within the system or from its environment. A system being studied to which no events occur is a static system; it has a single state. It is static in the sense that no event occurs that changes that state. Inanimate objects, composed of two or more elements, are familiar examples of static systems.

A dynamic system possesses more than one state and is referred to as a multi-state system. As events occur to a dynamic system, the system changes states because its structural properties change in response to the events as they occur. Any object that moves or any system that responds to its environment in any way is generally classed as a dynamic system. Events, as defined above, occur to a dynamic system, as compared to a static system in which no events occur because the system has only one state.

A system that maintains its state through a feedback cycle and a regulator of some type is a homeostatic system. A heating system, as in a home, that maintains a constant temperature is classed as a homeostatic system, as is the feature known as "cruise control" in some motor cars that maintains a constant speed regardless of the inclination of the road.

SYSTEMS BEHAVIOR

The behavior of a system becomes important when a system event initiates other events in the system or its environment. The manner in which a system responds is a means of classifying system behavior. The following definitions are relevant to system behavior:

1. "A *reaction* of a system is a system event for which another event that happens to the same system or its environment is sufficient."
2. "A *response* of a system is a system event for which another event that happens to the same system or to its environment is necessary but not sufficient, that is a system event produced by another system or environmental event (the *stimulus*)."
3. "An *act* of a system is a system event for the occurrence of

which no change in the system's environment is either necessary or sufficient."

Thus, when the occurrence of an event causes a system to behave in a deterministic manner, the system reacts solely to that event and no other event or stimulus is necessary for the determined event to occur. In a computer system, for example, a hardware detected machine error normally causes processing to be interrupted—regardless of the state of the processing unit. Clearly, other conditions can cause interruptions, so a machine error is a sufficient but not a necessary condition for an interruption to occur. In a system response, the system itself participates in the generation of the "response event," either through the current state of the system or through a supplementary condition that exists. Thus, in a computer system, an input/output interruption normally can occur only when the processing unit is enabled for input/output interruptions—that is, the processing unit is in a "necessary" state for the interruption to be accepted. An act is an event that is caused by the system itself and no event in the environment (of the system) is either necessary or sufficient. Using the previous examples, the execution of a computer instruction that causes an interruption to occur is an act since no external event is required.

SYSTEMS CLASSIFICATION BASED ON OBJECTIVES AND BEHAVIORAL PROPERTIES

The manner in which a system behaves can be used as a means of classification, provided that the classification also takes the objective of the system into consideration. The following definitions are relevant to system classification:

1. "A *state-maintaining system* is one that (1) can react in only one way to any one external or internal event; but (2) it reacts differently to different external or internal events; and (3) these different reactions produce the same external or internal state (outcome)."
2. "A *goal-seeking system* is one that can respond differently to one or more different external or internal events in one or more different external or internal states and that can respond differently to a particular event in an unchanging environment until it produces a particular state (outcome)."

3. "A *purposeful system* is one which can produce the same outcome in different ways in the same (internal or external) state and can produce different outcomes in the same and different states."
4. "The *goal* of a purposeful system in a particular situation is a preferred outcome that can be obtained within a specified time period."
5. "The *objective* of a purposeful system in a particular situation is a preferred outcome that cannot be obtained within a specified period but which can be obtained over a longer time period."
6. "The *function(s)* of a system is production of the outcomes that define its goal(s) and objectives(s)."
7. "A system is *adaptive* if, when there is a change in its environmental and/or internal state which reduces its efficiency in pursuing one or more of the goals that define its function(s), it reacts or responds by changing its own state and/or that of its environment so as to increase its efficiency with respect to that goal or goals."

Characteristically, a state-maintaining system is adaptive and possesses the following capabilities:

1. The capability of sensing its environment and distinguishing between different values.
2. A feedback cycle that permits the system to "react" to the stimulus by changing its state to achieve the desired state of the system.

Thus, a heating system or a cruise control feature is a state-maintaining system because its objective is to place the system in a desired state; it is adaptive because as the desired state is approached, less energy is applied. One of the most significant characteristics of a state-maintaining system is that it can react in only one way to an event. (Note the word "react" in the preceding sentence.) In a heating system, if the thermostat detects an ambient room temperature that is less than the temperature setting, it causes heat to be applied to and greater or lesser degree. If the ambient room temperature is greater than or equal to the temperature setting, then the heat is turned off. In most heating systems of this type, air conditioning is *not* turned on for the "greater than" case. This is character-istic of a state-maintaining system. Similarly, the cruise control feature in a motor car can cause the throttle to be applied or not to be applied, depending upon the speed of the car and the speed setting. It does not cause the braking system to be actuated when the speed of the car becomes too great. This is one of the reasons that most car manuals state that cruise control should be used only over a given speed, such as 50 miles per hour.

In a *goal-seeking system*, energy is applied to achieve a given state and the manner in which the system responds is dependent upon the event and the internal state. Familiar examples of goal-seeking systems are the automatic temperature control in a motor car and the autopilot in an aircraft. In a motor car, equipped with the above feature, either heat or air conditioning is applied, depending upon the ambient temperature and the temperature setting. Thus, the system responds by making a decision as to which form of energy to apply. (Note the word "respond" in the preceding sentence.) Thus, the system can respond differently to a given ambient temperature. The same analysis applies to an autopilot that is set to hold a given azimuth and altitude. Thus, when an aircraft deviates from the goal, energy is applied to cause the aircraft to make a change of "yaw" or "pitch," depending upon the nature of the deviation.

The terms "goal" and "objective" apply to systems that possess intelligence, which generally means that they are purposeful systems. A system of this type can select shorter-term goals to achieve a longer-term objective. Human systems are usually classed as being purposeful; however, the area of research known as "artificial intelli-gence" or "machine intelligence" has produced purposeful systems for specific types of behavior.

CONCLUSION

Clearly, there is much more to the study of systems than the twenty definitions given here. In fact, Ackoff's original paper contains thirty-two varied and sundry definitions with an appropriate dis-cussion of each one. However, the objective of providing a means of communication has been achieved. Systems thinking requires a more specific definition of a system other than the fact that it is a set of elements. Supposedly, Eskimos can differentiate between one hundred kinds of snow and the difference is apparently significant in their modes of communication. The same concept would apply to the study of systems.

REFERENCES

Ackoff, R. L., "Towards a system of systems concepts," *Management Science*, Volume 17, No. 11 (July, 1971), pp. 661–671.
Emery, F. E. (Editor), *Systems Thinking*, Baltimore, Penguin Books, 1969.
Hall, A. D., *A Methodology for Systems Engineering*, New York, Van Nostrand Reinhold Company, 1962.

3 | SYSTEM DEVELOPMENT LIFE CYCLE

INTRODUCTION

Most systems evolve through a set of successive stages from initial conception of the system idea to final cessation of system utilization. The set of stages is known as the *system life cycle*, and a high degree of commonalty exists between the stages of development of different systems, especially in the areas of computers, data processing, and information systems. Rubin* lists the eight stages in the system life cycle as:

1. Conception.
2. Preliminary analysis.
3. System design.
4. Programming.
5. System documentation.
6. System installation.
7. System operation.
8. System cessation.

Stage numbered four, entitled "programming," relates to computer-

*Rubin, p. 4.

based systems; if it were replaced by an activity generally known as "development" or "implementation," then the set of stages would apply to systems development activity in a general fashion.

To a large degree, the above stages only approximate real life and serve as a model for organization and planning. For example, the class of activities known in operations research as "controlling and implementing the solution"* is not included in the system life cycle. The practicalities of system development are such that the solution (i.e., system) must be monitored and controlled because it may lose some of its effectiveness due to changes in the operating environment. The process of monitoring and controlling the effectiveness of a system necessarily involves a feedback cycle, which is not included in Rubin's system life cycle. The need for monitoring and control may become necessary as a result of three possible conditions:

1. A previously irrelevant system variable may become relevant.
2. The value of one or more system variables may change and affect the operational logic of the system.
3. The functional components of the system may change or need to be adjusted.

Thus, the feedback cycle is a practical reality that can be viewed both from within the life cycle and from outside the life cycle in its operating environment. As a result, the design and documentation methodology does not include methods for describing this aspect of the system development life cycle, even though systems themselves include feedback that can be described with the HIPO technique.

CONCEPTION

The conception stage is used to determine whether or not a need exists for the new system. The need can be recognized by the system design and development group (e.g., the data processing department) or by the organization that the new system is expected to service. In the latter case, the manager involved is usually aware of a need, but is not certain that a new or improved system is feasible.

The conception stage is formalized when the systems department and the operational group meet to identify the specific need and to

---

*For example, see Churchman, et al., pp. 595–622.

determine whether the systems approach supports the goals of the organization.

When a new system is to exist as a product or service, the conception stage represents a preliminary market analysis and a summarization of the relevant business conditions. In organizations that normally deal in products and services, ideas for "new business" occur frequently and the conception stage serves to sort out ideas that warrant further study. The conception stage is summarized in a convenient form in Figure 3.1.

The result of the conception stage of the system life cycle is normally a report to the sponsoring department that summarizes the needs, resources, and other pertinent information about the proposed system. The report serves as a medium for deciding whether to pursue the proposed system development effort or to drop the idea altogether.

PRELIMINARY ANALYSIS

Preliminary analysis is popularly known as the "feasibility study" and is primarily concerned with three areas:

1. The characteristics of the present system or operating environment.
2. Consideration of whether a new system should be developed or the present system should be revised.
3. Whether the proposed system is viable for the sponsoring organization.

Even though the preliminary analysis function is commonly performed by a systems analyst, it is usually assisted through management participation by the sponsoring organization, either through direct participation or by permitting the analyst to work through members of the sponsoring organization. Figure 3.2 gives an overview diagram of the preliminary design stage of the system life cycle.

Inputs to the preliminary design stage are listed as follows:

1. Characteristics of the current system (i.e., the existing system if one exists).
2. Ideas for the proposed system.
3. Organization factors.
4. Financial considerations.

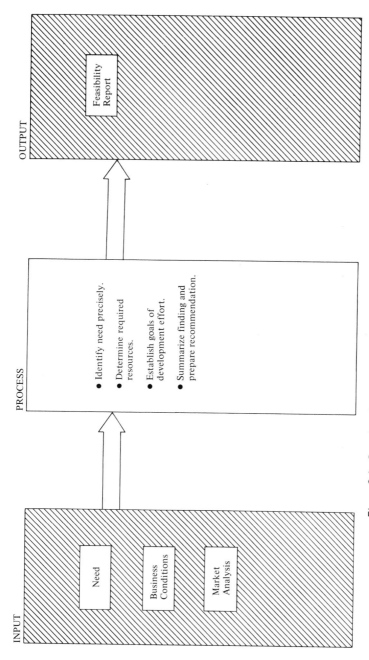

Figure 3.1 Overview diagram of the conception stage of the system life cycle.

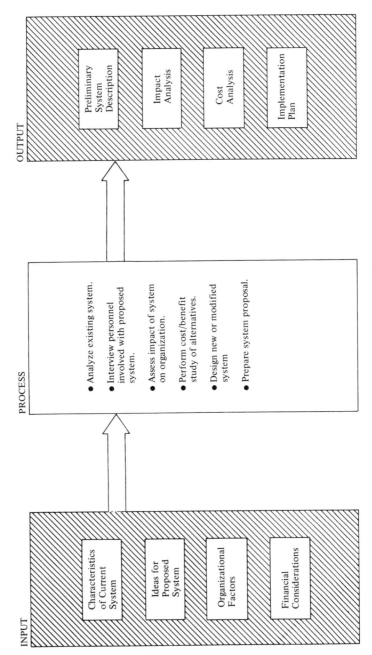

Figure 3.2   Overview diagram of the preliminary design stage of the system life cycle.

Characteristics of the current system are determined through existing documentation, and in the event that it does not exist, through extensive analysis by the systems analyst. This is the first instance in the system life cycle in which effective documentation of the existing system is important for ongoing analysis. Clearly, detailed documentation is not necessary, but a general description of the system at the "overview" level is required. *Ideas for the proposed system* are obtained by the analyst as a separate step or as a by-product of the need to document the existing system. This step is particularly significant when proposed changes to an existing system are planned. In many cases, actual users of a system are the only ones that are aware of its deficiencies. It is also important to recognize that many, if not most, users of a system are unaware of the potentialities of a new system, especially in the case of computer-based systems, and tend to express needs, limitations, and deficiencies in their own language. (Thus, the analyst must also be a translator.) *Organization factors*, which unfortunately are ignored in many cases, include: organizational politics, resistance to change, previous (bad) experience with systems work, and the type of employees involved. Organizational factors can "make or break" a systems effort if left unrecognized, but generally do not result in organizational problems if considered during the preliminary analysis state. *Financial considerations* normally include the cost of the current system and standard implementation costs. In the latter case, expected implementation costs are used to determine how much the proposed system development effort will cost in terms of the organization's resources.

The objective of the preliminary analysis stage is to investigate the feasibility of developing a system to satisfy the needs identified during the system conception stage, and if a new or modified system is both desirable and practical, to propose an effective system that satisfies the stated needs. The functions performed in the preliminary analysis stage usually include:

1. *Analyze* existing system.
2. *Interview* personnel involved with the proposed system.
3. *Assess* impact of new or modified system on the organization.
4. *Perform* cost/benefit study of alternatives.
5. *Design* new or modified system.
6. *Prepare* system proposal.

188532

The specific functions performed by the analyst during the preliminary analysis stage are self-explanatory and are not discussed further. (The reader is referred to a reference on the system life cycle, such as Rubin* or Benjamin†.) It should be mentioned, however, that an *implementation plan* is necessary for the system design and development stages, because of its importance in the success or failure of a systems effort, and this plan is an output of the feasibility study. When data processing is involved in the systems evaluation, then a special effort should be made to determine the optimum resolution of the problem rather than the course of action that would invariably lead to automation. Clearly, the feasibility study may simply reinforce the use of manual procedures.

The outputs of the preliminary analysis stage are:

1. A preliminary system description.
2. An impact analysis.
3. A cost analysis.
4. An implementation plan.

Each of the four outputs is important, but can realistically be presented to management at different times, depending upon organizational factors. The *preliminary system description* along with the cost analysis are the primary inputs to the management decision-making process and effectively determine whether a proposal is accepted or rejected. The two main reasons that systems proposals are accepted by organizational management are increased functional capability and reduced cost. At this point, management is concerned with function and not specific design details, and many proposals are rejected solely on the basis of cost because the functional capability of the system is not clearly understood. In short, the analyst is presenting structure and implementation rather than function. Required equipment and personnel can be included either in the preliminary system specification or in the cost analysis. *Impact analysis* concerns the effect of the proposed system upon organizational operations, or in the case of a product or service, justification for the proposed system in the form of a competitive analysis. *Cost analysis* includes both development costs and operational costs, in addition to a summarization of current costs in the case of an in-house system. In the case of

*Rubin, *op cit.*, pp. 19–59.
†Benjamin.

a product or service, the cost analysis would necessarily include expected return on investment, a cost/value analysis, and a study of any risk factors that are involved. The *implementation plan* is intended to summarize needed resources and establish dates and schedules. In short, the implementation plan outlines the remainder of the system life cycle for management comments, suggestions, and approval.

From the viewpoint of system description and documentation, the preliminary analysis stage of the system life cycle is the first that is dependent upon descriptive techniques. At this stage, the required level of detail includes only an overview diagram at the uppermost level in the hierarchy diagram. However, this is where effective documentation originates—at the preliminary analysis stage of system development.

SYSTEM DESIGN

The system design stage of the system cycle is concerned with the hierarchical structure of the system and the functions that are performed at each level and by each component of the system. The system design effort utilizes the preliminary system description, developed during the feasibility study, and molds that description into a set of design specifications that can be used during the development stage.

System design involves five major functions:

1. The analysis of system objectives and the respecification of these objectives as design constraints.
2. The investigation of possible modes of system operation and requirements for physical facilities.
3. The establishment of the operational capability of the system and physical equipment needed.
4. The specification of the functional structure of the system and the development of a precise description of each system component.
5. Documentation of the design of the system.

Figure 3.3 gives an overview diagram of the design stage of the system life cycle.

Input to the design stage includes four major items:

1. The preliminary system description, mentioned above.

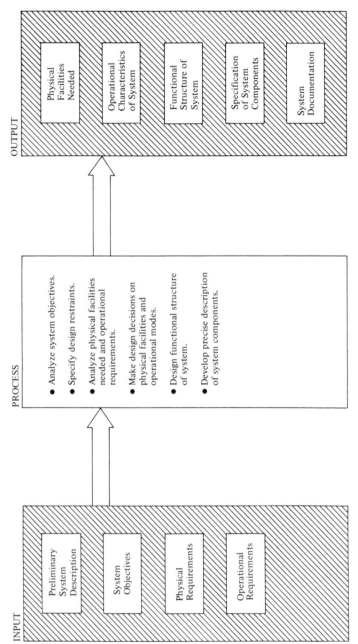

Figure 3.3   Overview diagram of the design stage of the system life cycle.

2. A set of system objectives.
3. Physical requirements.
4. Operational requirements.

The set of *system objectives* governs the design of a system and serves to aid in insuring that the system that management decided upon is the same system that will be produced. The objectives may be contained in the preliminary system description or they may be developed by the system designer. The system objectives may also specify the inputs and outputs of the system, although perhaps at a relatively high level. In a data processing system, for example, an objective might be to generate a particular type of management report, which may implicitly dictate that a particular kind of information system be developed from which that report can be obtained.

The task of determining the necessary modes of system operation and the required physical facilities may require an investigation by the system designer of the possible modes in which the system can operate and the equipment needed to sustain that type of operation. The investigation may additionally include a study of how inputs to the system will be obtained and how outputs will be used. The investigation phase can be conducted through interviews, questionnaires, and reports. To sum up, if the necessary inputs to the design stage are not available beforehand, then the designer must obtain them himself.

Design decisions regarding physical facilities and operational requirements are based on the preliminary system description, design objectives, and the information obtained in the investigation of physical and operational capabilities. Physical facilities depend upon the system involved but characteristically take the form of computer and storage requirements, physical space needed, vehicles that will be available, etc. Operational capabilities involve the manner in which the physical facilities are used and typically involve how information will be organized and accessed. The physical and operational specifications for a system are established in this step; these specifications serve as the external description of the system.

The process of specifying the functional structure of a system that provides the required operational capability through the physical facilities is referred to as "systems design." Normally, the hierarchical structure of the components that comprise the system is given and each component is described in detail. The inputs, outputs, and internal logic of each component are defined. Internal logic is usually described with equations, flow diagrams, or decision tables, and the system, as a whole, is described with a general "system" flow diagram or a HIPO diagram. Clearly, the internal logic of a component utilizes the design decisions established previously that concern physical facilities, operational capabilities, and information structures.

Effective documentation of a system starts at the design stage—and perhaps earlier as the preliminary system description. The objective of documentation at the design level is to give the implementation group something to work with and to provide management with the needed information for decision making. Clearly, documentation is an important by-product of the design phase and not an effort that takes place after the project has been completed. Another factor that is frequently included in all phases of system design, especially documentation, is a description of the physical environment in which the system is intended to operate.

The design cycle normally includes feedback between the prospective user of the system and the system designer. This type of feedback is healthy and helps to insure that systems are not designed in a vacuum. After the system design phase has been completed, the prospective user of the system should have a set of specifications that are understandable and acceptable to him, and at the same time, are technically practical and satisfy the stated objectives of the system. The same set of specifications serve as input to the implementation stage.

SYSTEM IMPLEMENTATION

The system implementation stage is the one in which the logic and specifications of a system are put to the test of a realistic development effort. Briefly stated, the integrity of the system design is verified. An accepted practice is for the development team to hold "structured walkthroughs," in which the logic of the system is subjected to the scrutiny of the development team in a face-to-face environment.

The precise nature of the implementation stage is necessarily dependent upon the type of system being developed. In hardware systems development, detailed logic diagrams for the components of the system are constructed before the components are built. After each component is built, it is subjected to a functional test to insure that it operates according to specifications. The various components of a system are assembled according to a preestablished plan and the complete system is "system tested" to insure that the interfaces between the components are properly designed and that the system meets its operational objectives.

In the implementation of computer software systems, detail diagrams of each component are constructed and the design specifications are implemented as software modules. Each module is unit tested, to insure that it functions properly, prior to integration of the modules of the system. The complete system is then system tested, as mentioned above. During software systems implementation, software modules are associated with detail diagrams.

Software systems development has evolved as a bottom-to-top process wherein the "lower-level" modules in the hierarchical structure of a system are implemented before "higher-level" modules, as suggested in Figure 3.4. The difficulties with bottom-to-top development are that many module interfaces must be developed simultaneously, often by more than one person, and that a driver program must be developed to perform the unit testing of a module. Bottom-to-top development is error-prone, because of the module interfaces, and integration of modules to form a complete system is cumbersome because of the fact that all modules must "come together" at the same time.

An alternate approach to systems implementation is to use top-down development, as suggested in Figure 3.5. Top-down development is considered by many professionals to be superior to bottom-to-top development because modules are developed in a natural order from the control structures downward. No driver programs are required and the concept of a stub is employed to test module interfaces. A stub is simply a short module that displays a message stating that program control reached that module and then returns to the calling program. One of the primary advantages of top-down development is that the system is always operable, so an integration effort is not required as the last stage of implementation.

Systems implementation also applies to "people systems" in which detailed logic diagrams or detailed module descriptions are replaced by detailed job descriptions. In many human systems, implementation takes the form of reorganization of the management system.

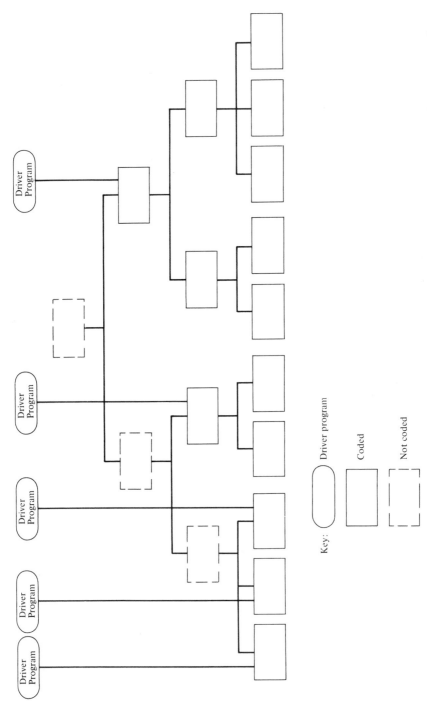

Figure 3.4   A conceptual view of a bottom-to-top development, showing the hierarchical structure of the system and driver programs for testing purposes.

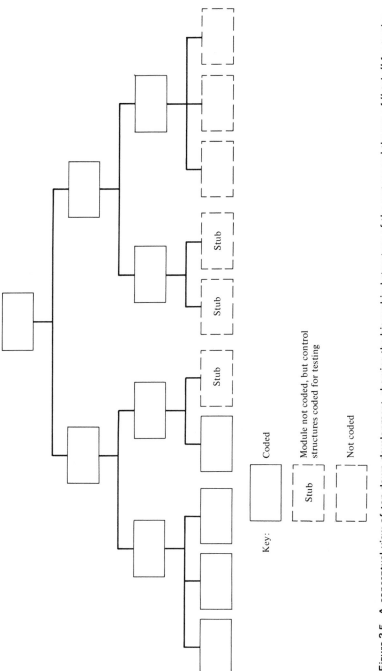

Key:

Coded

Stub — Module not coded, but control structures coded for testing

Not coded

Figure 3.5 A conceptual view of top-down development, showing the hierarchical structure of the system and the use of "stubs" for testing.

Interestingly enough, component and module interfaces in hardware and software systems are analogous to people interfaces in human systems and the system testing phase of hardware and software systems corresponds to the period in human systems in which the informal structure of a management system is developed.

In the implementation of most systems, there is a considerable amount of feedback between the development effort and the system designers. This is usually a result of the fact that unforeseen circumstances arise and the design of the system must be adjusted accordingly. The need for feedback and adjustment also arises out of limitations in the design of a system, so the implementation stage can also serve as a check on the integrity of the system.

SYSTEM DOCUMENTATION

System documentation is the set of documents that provide general and detailed information on the system. In general, effective documentation is necessary for installing, maintaining, and using a system and for ongoing analysis of the system's performance. Documentation should satisfy four needs:

1. As a reference for management.
2. As a reference for design, implementation, and maintenance personnel.
3. As a reference for operators of the system—in the case of hardware or software systems.
4. As a reference for users of the system.

Unfortunately, system documentation is frequently regarded as a discrete stage in the system life cycle, whereas in reality, effective documentation is achieved by applying a technically sound methodology at the conception, preliminary analysis, design, and implementation stages of the system life cycle, and by "putting it all together" during the documentation stage.

The HIPO technique is effective for needs numbered one and two, since the components of a HIPO package provide a means of describing a system at varying levels of detail. A HIPO package must be supplemented with the following types of information when used in an organizational environment:

1. An outline of the departments involved and the responsibilities of the departments affected.

2. A specification of the inputs to the system that must be supplied by the user and an explanation of the meaning of the outputs of the system.
3. A manual of operating procedures for the operator of the system, whenever appropriate, and a precise description of the action to be taken under special conditions.

Normally, documentation methods include verbal descriptions, syntactical specifications, list of rules, flow diagrams, and decision tables—in addition to the HIPO diagrams—and depend upon the type of system being described. In computer software systems, programs can also be self-documenting provided that a set of programming conventions are supplied to the programmer and he is required to adhere to the rules. Similarly, logic diagrams, engineering drawings, and schematics are also a means of documenting hardware systems.

SYSTEM INSTALLATION, OPERATION, AND CESSATION

System installation, operation, and cessation are the final three stages in the system life cycle. *System installation* refers to the process of putting a system into operation and the activity related to passing shake-down and acceptance tests. In a computer and data processing environment, system installation may also refer to the conversion of data formats to meet the needs of the new system and the adjustment of operating procedures. System installation frequently involves training and demonstrations. Clearly, training usually refers to operations personnel and emphasizes the operational characteristics of the new or modified system. Demonstrations are usually management-oriented and serve to orient the organization with the added capability that is provided with the new system and the impact the new system will have on the day-to-day operations in the organization.

System operation refers to the operation of the new or modified system after installation has been completed. Optimally, the system should be monitored during the initial operational period to insure that the system designers have "zeroed in" on the system needed by the organization. Operator's manuals should be reviewed for accuracy and completeness, and operational standards should be established.

System cessation refers to the practical eventuality that all systems have a finite life, and are either replaced or modified as the operational environment evolves. Because of the reality that system cessation does exist, a system should be controlled and monitored so that the need for replacement or modification is recognized with enough lead time to insure that continued operation of the system does not degrade the performance of the organization. Monitoring for system cessation differs from monitoring of the system during the initial period of operation. The analysis exists at a higher level; in fact, system cessation may actually be a part of the implementation plan developed earlier in the system life cycle.

To sum up, system installation includes training of operators *and* prospective users, acceptance testing, orientation of the organization to the new system, and demonstration of the capability of the new or modified system. System operation is concerned with operational procedures, monitoring, performance evaluation, and standards. Lastly, system cessation is concerned with the ongoing analysis of a system's contribution to the objectives of an organization.

CONCLUSIONS

There is a definite orientation of the system life cycle to the computer field and the systems analysis function with an organizational environment. However, because of the commonality of systems, as covered in Chapter 1, the concepts apply in general.

Regardless of the type of system involved, system design and documentation plays a major role in most stages of the system life cycle, and serves as the primary vehicle for passing information between the various stages. Descriptive techniques include verbal descriptions, syntactical specifications, logic diagrams, drawings and schematics, flow diagrams, and decision tables, to name only the most widely used techniques. To this list, we add the HIPO technique which spans several of the stages in the system life cycle and replaces the need, in many cases, for other descriptive techniques.

REFERENCES

Benjamin, R. I., *Control of the Information System Development Cycle*, New York, John Wiley & Sons, Inc., 1970.

Churchman, C. W., R. L. Ackoff, and E. L. Arnoff, *Introduction to Operations Research*, New York, John Wiley and Sons, Inc., 1957.

Couger, J. D., and R. W. Knapp (editors), *System Analysis Techniques*, New York, John Wiley and Sons, Inc., 1974.

Rubin, M. L., *Handbook of Data Processing Management, Volume 1, Introduction to the System Life Cycle*, Princeton, Brandon/Systems Press, 1970.

4 | INTRODUCTION TO THE HIPO TECHNIQUE

INTRODUCTION

The HIPO technique was developed in the computer industry to display, in a graphical manner, what a system or program does and what data it uses and creates. As such, HIPO can be used as a design aid and as a documentation tool. When the HIPO technique is used, the description of a system can be used throughout the life cycle of that system. Thus, the documentation of a system is generated as a by-product of the design and implementation phases and not solely as a separate phase in the system life cycle. Certainly, a formal step called "documentation" is still important in the system life cycle. However, using the HIPO technique, documentation is only finalized in the documentation phase; it originates with the beginning of the system development life cycle.

The Need for Improved Techniques

HIPO represents a *new* technique for describing systems. Conventional methods such as flow diagrams, decision tables, and words are frequently ineffective for operational reasons. During systems design, conventional techniques are used, typically, to give only the structure of a system so that designers and implementors are collectively "working in the dark," as far as function is concerned. Designers are commonly concerned over whether a system has a "hole" in it. What this means is that frequently it is not known until the testing phase if the system is lacking in a needed functional capability. Thus, a neglected operational function that has been "missed" during design and implementation and discovered during testing may cause unnecessary rework and modification and could result in slipped schedules and cost overruns. During systems modification, it is difficult to get at the source of a problem in a large and complex system because needed modifications are given in functional terms and the usual documentation describes the structure of a system. An excessive amount of time is spent looking for needed information about a system in order to isolate the component that must be modified.

The basic problem is that most documentation is in words with accompanying flow diagrams and decision tables, and as such is concerned with the elements that comprise the system. However, when an operational capability is required, the person using that capability (i.e., the problem originator) deals only with the function that is performed and not with *how* it is performed. Thus, the systems person is required to translate function into structure, logic, and organization—a feat that may be very difficult if the system is large and complex.

The Functional Approach

The HIPO technique is intended to show function because designers design function and implementors (e.g., programmers) implement and modify function. Most existing methods for describing systems, which emphasize structure, are inadequate for decision making at the systems level because decision makers are mainly concerned with the function of a system. The reason is straightforward. The actual systems development process is generally considered to be a specialized technique that begins with a specification of the needed functional capability and produces the internal structure of a system as part of its developmental activity. It is outside of the domain of most decision makers.

Once we have a method for describing the function of a system, however, it is readily apparent that the technology can be transferred to systems that are not exclusively computer or data processing

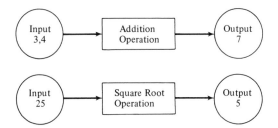

Figure 4.1 Commonly used arithmetic operations are classed as functions.

oriented. Most systems that are developed in the course of human activity are open in the sense that they interact with their environment. The HIPO technique is particularly relevant to describing open systems and their components which may also be systems, because it permits the inputs, processes, and outputs of the system to be specified. The inputs and outputs describe how a component interacts with its environment; the processes describe what the component does.

It must be emphasized that HIPO can be used only to describe function, and not structure, logic, and organization. All systems possess a formal organization which may or may not be functionally oriented. When HIPO is used as a design technique, formal organization tends to reflect the functional orientation of the system.   In most, but not all, cases this is a desirable attribute.

The Concept of a Function

A function is conveniently defined as a process that accepts one or more inputs and produces one or more outputs. The commonly known arithmetic operations and the square root function in mathematics are familiar examples of functions, as depicted in Figure 4.1. More specifically, as suggested by Figure 4.2, a function is a mapping between two sets: the set of inputs and the set of outputs.* Thus, the HIPO technique is relevant to describing function because it lists the inputs and outputs and also describes the process involved in accepting input and generating output.   When HIPO is used, the

---

*Mathematicians also recognize functions without an input set (niladic) and without an output set. Clearly, a system can also exhibit the same characteristics. Some organizations, for example, are accused of accepting no input and others are faulted for not generating any output.

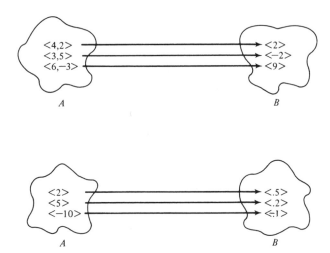

Figure 4.2 Formally, a function is a mapping between two sets. In this case, the function is $f(A) \rightarrow B$ for the minus and reciprocal operations, respectively.

traditional functional description that shows inputs and outputs is supplemented with a hierarchy diagram that gives the functional breakdown of the system and shows how the functional components fit together.

THE HIPO PACKAGE

A HIPO package is a means of describing a system or program by subdividing the function of that system or program in a meaningful manner. A typical HIPO package consists of the following components:

1. A visual table of contents.
2. Overview diagrams.
3. Detail diagrams with extended descriptions.

The *visual table of contents* is similar to an organization chart and gives the hierarchical structure of the functions that comprise a system or program. *Overview diagrams* provide a means of describing the inputs, processes, and outputs for the major functions in an application. *Detail diagrams* with extended descriptions show specific functions but point to implementation that takes the form of actual routines, flow diagrams, and supporting text. The relationship among the components in a HIPO package is given in the first chapter.

Input-Process-Output Diagrams

The input-process-output diagram, which is the basis of a HIPO package, is shown conceptually in Figure 4.3. The box on the left lists the inputs to a particular function and the box on the right lists the outputs of that function. The box in the middle lists the steps that comprise the function and in the case of high-level diagrams, the steps point to lower-level diagrams. Figure 4.4 gives an input-process-output diagram for a charge account processing system that could apply to an automated or nonautomated environment. If an input-process-output diagram represents an overview diagram, then each step in the process would be further described by a lower-level overview or detail diagram. If an input-process-output diagram represents a detail diagram, then each step in the process would be supported by an entry in an extended description that might point to actual implementation, that is represented by flow diagrams, decision tables, and possibly a computer program.

Visual Table of Contents

The objective of the visual table of contents is to supply a top-down functional breakdown of a system or program. Each box in the hierarchy diagram corresponds to an input-process-output diagram that describes the corresponding function along with its input and output sets. Figure 4.5 depicts a typical visual table of contents for a credit/billing system that involves manual procedures and computer data processing.

The visual table of contents is comprised of three components:

1. A hierarchy diagram.
2. A legend.
3. An optional description section.

The major component is the hierarchy diagram that contains the names and identification numbers of overview and detail diagrams in the HIPO package. The hierarchy diagram serves as an organization chart of a system or a program; each function is broken down into subfunctions in the same fashion that business organizations

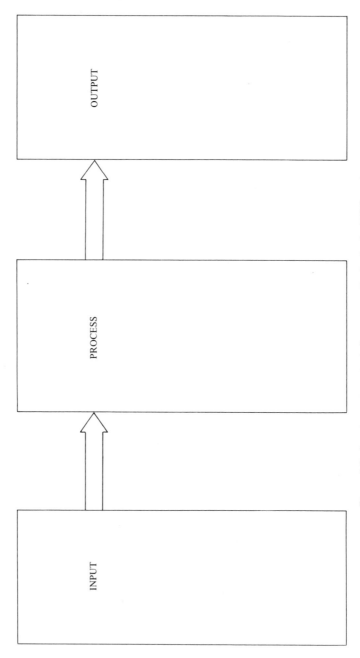

Figure 4.3   Input-process-output diagrams are the basis of a HIPO package.

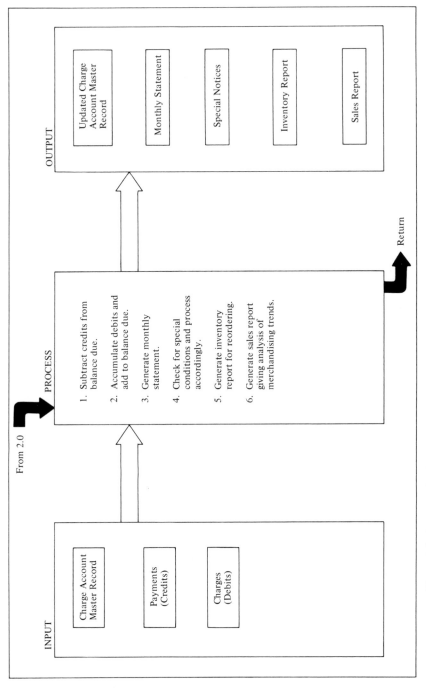

Figure 4.4   An example of an input-process-output diagram for a typical charge account processing system.

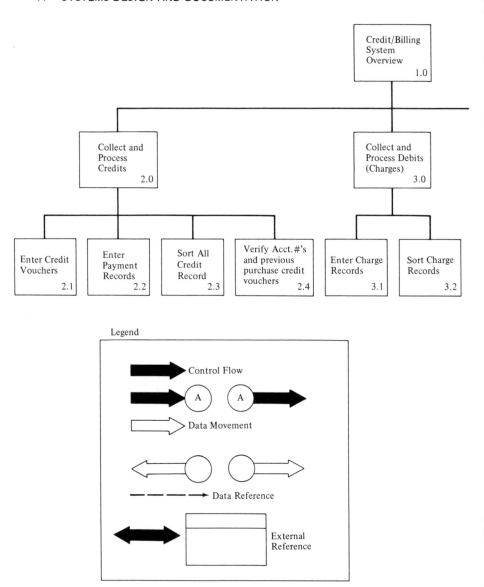

Figure 4.5   Visual table of contents.

are broken down into divisions, departments, groups, etc. A person using or reading a HIPO package can obtain a functional description of a component at varying levels of detail by following the chain from the highest functional level down through one or more subfunctions. Thus, the reader need not search through the complete

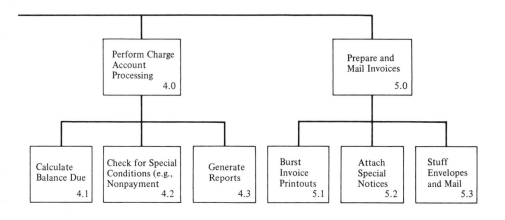

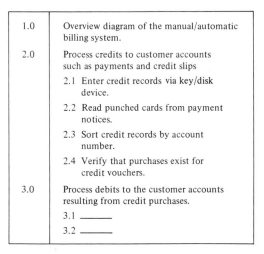

1.0	Overview diagram of the manual/automatic billing system.
2.0	Process credits to customer accounts such as payments and credit slips
	2.1 Enter credit records via key/disk device.
	2.2 Read punched cards from payment notices.
	2.3 Sort credit records by account number.
	2.4 Verify that purchases exist for credit vouchers.
3.0	Process debits to the customer accounts resulting from credit purchases.
	3.1 ————
	3.2 ————

Figure 4.5 *(Continued)*

set of input-process-output diagrams to locate the description of a needed function. All that is required is to locate the particular box in the hierarchy diagram, *at the desired level of detail*; the box will contain an identification number of an overview diagram or a detailed diagram that describes the function or subfunction in more detail.

A hierarchy diagram should be read from left to right at a given level of detail to determine what the system does. At the given level, the outputs of a functional component serve as input, if appropriate, to the functional component on its immediate right. If it is necessary to obtain additional information, then the user of the hierarchy diagram should drop down successive levels until the required detail is available. To sum up, a hierarchy diagram is analyzed from left to right to determine what the system or program does, it is searched from top to bottom to obtain information on a particular functional component. The two main uses of the hierarchy diagram are conceptualized in Figure 4.6.

The *legend* of the visual table of contents (see Figure 4.5) lists the symbols used in the HIPO package and tells how they are used. While a standard set of symbols would ordinarily be used, the legend serves as a reference for persons who do not use HIPO diagrams on a regular basis. Another consideration is that descriptive techniques tend to evolve so that with a legend, a complete package would be meaningful at a later date, regardless of the current standards at that time. The later point is particularly relevant for the documentation of computer programs; it is customary for a program to be modified after it has been in production for several months or years when the analyst and programmer that were responsible for its development are no longer available. Even though the standards may have evolved, the legend reflects the meaning of those symbols when the HIPO package was written.

The optional *description section* provides more information on each function than can be contained in each box. Normally, each box in the hierarchy contains only the title of a diagram and its identification number which points the reader to an overview or detail diagram. Therefore, the description section allows the reader to obtain additional information on a diagram without actually going to that diagram. Each entry in the description section is a one or two sentence description of the corresponding box in the hierarchy diagram.

Overview Diagrams

The purpose of an overview diagram is to provide a general idea of the function to be performed at a particular stage of a system or

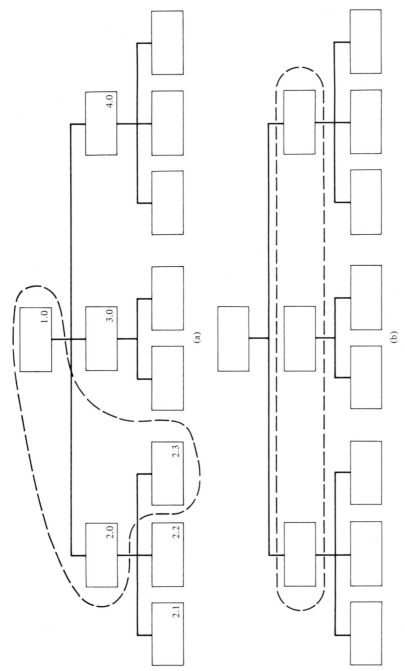

Figure 4.6 The hierarchy diagram can be used (a) to locate a particular component; or (b) to understand a system or program at a given level of detail.

application. Normally, a specific overview diagram is located through the hierarchy diagram in the visual table of contents. An overview diagram takes the form of an input-process-output diagram; the inputs are listed at the left and the outputs are listed on the right. The key characteristic of an overview diagram is its generality. There is no indication of how and where the inputs are used and how and where the outputs are generated. The process block in the middle of the overview diagram describes "what" functions are performed, but does not tell "how" they are performed. The input-process-output diagram in Figure 4.4 is an overview diagram; it can be identified, as indicated previously, by two defining characteristics:

1. The inputs, outputs, and steps of the process are simply listed.
2. There is no explicit indication of where the inputs are used and how the outputs are generated.

Another example of an overview diagram is given in Figure 4.7 which depicts the functions that might be performed in a computer program for processing automobile insurance policies.

The steps in the process block of an overview diagram normally correspond to lower-level overview diagrams or to detail diagrams, and represent subfunctions in the hierarchy diagram of the visual table of contents. When a step in the process block *does* represent a subfunction, it can be enclosed in a box with a number in the lower right-hand corner of the box. This number is the identification number of the next lower overview or detail diagram that describes the subfunction.

Detail Diagrams

The purpose of a detail diagram is to give a simple and brief description of a particular function. Specific inputs and outputs are identified and they are associated with the steps in the process block that use them. Whereas input and output sets for overview diagrams designate files and sometimes records, input and output sets for detail diagrams frequently represent records and fields within records.

An example of a detail diagram is given as Figure 4.8. The diagram represents a typical banking procedure wherein canceled checks are magnetically encoded with the dollar amount of the check and entered into the computer system for processing. In this example,

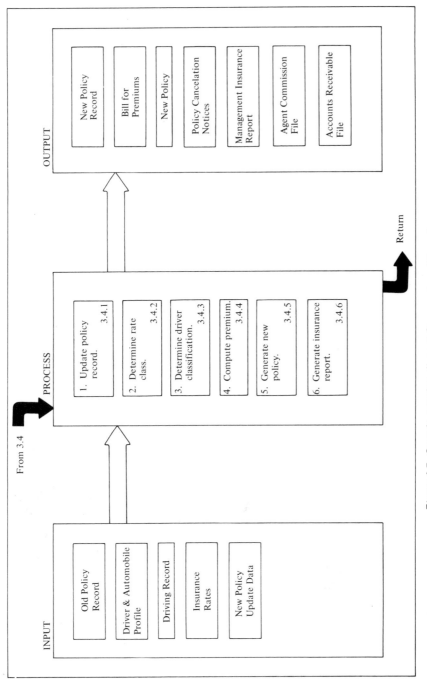

Figure 4.7   Sample overview diagram for an automobile policy program.

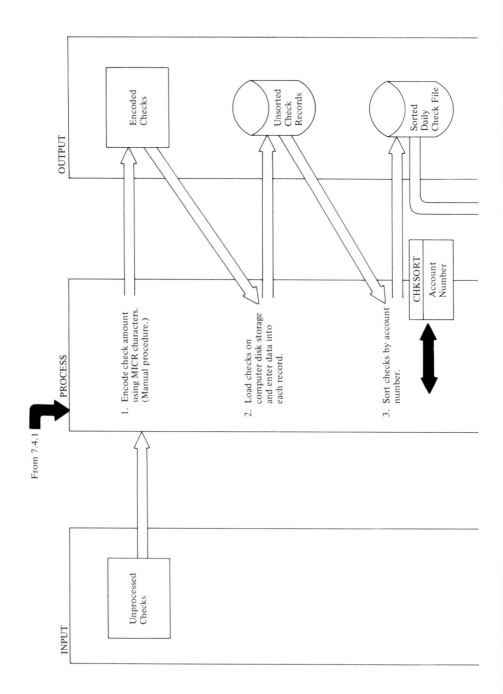

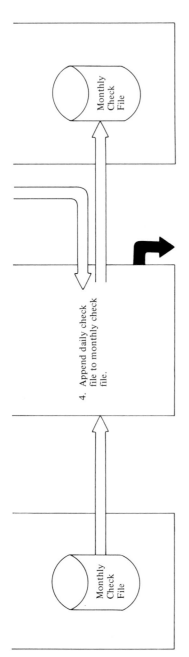

Notes	Routine	Label	Flow Chart	Ref.
1. Manually encode check amount using MICR recorder.				7.4.1.1
2. Read checks into storage, verify account number, append date, and write records to disk storage.	CHKLOAD	ENTER	CHK7.4.1	7.4.1.2
3. Sort checks using CHKSORT or account number.	CHKLOAD	SORT		7.4.1.3
4. Search to end of monthly check file and copy file. (File is sorted daily by date and account number.)	CHKLOAD	START	CHK7.4.2	7.4.1.4

Extended Description

Figure 4.8 Detail diagram for a preliminary bank check processing procedure.

the relationship of inputs and outputs to the steps in the process block is given specifically since the objective of the detail diagram is to show how the details fit together and serve as a cross reference to implementation. The process block of a detail diagram may also exhibit the use of external and internal subroutines, as in step 3 in Figure 4.8 which uses a sort routine named CHKSORT.

A detail diagram points to implementation through an *extended description* that contains an entry for each step in the process block. Although the contents of each entry in the extended description are arbitrary, a typical set of items might be:

1. A *note item* giving additional information on that step.
2. A *routine name* giving the program name that performs the specified function, in a computer environment, or the name of a job description or entry in a procedures manual, in a noncomputer environment.
3. A *label* that identifies the starting position in a routine, performing that function.
4. A *flow chart* reference that points to a detailed flow diagram for the step in the process.
5. An optional *reference* to the specific step in the process block.

The detail diagram should not show logic, and should exist as a *simple* and *brief* description of a particular function. If a detail diagram does depict logic, then the description has "gone too far" and shows implementation.

The amount of detail that is shown in a detail diagram is dependent upon the function being described. Overview and then detail diagrams go from the general to the specific, as reflected in the hierarchy diagram in the visual table of contents, and if knowledge of a particular field or item of information is necessary for describing a function, then it should be included in a detail diagram. The key point is that only the information necessary to understand a function should be included in the detail diagram; extraneous information confuses the issue and tends to make the diagram harder to understand.

To sum up, the objective of a HIPO package is to communicate— at all levels of detail. As the documentation goes from the general to the specific, as reflected in the hierarchy diagram, the description becomes more dependent upon implementation and points to implementation through the extended description. From the point of view of communication, the practice of describing function and not implementation is a sound one. Implementation may change because of new hardware, different languages and software, and because of the personnel involved. But function usually remains the same.

DEVELOPMENT OF A HIPO PACKAGE

The use of HIPO is an operational technique that can be employed throughout the life cycle of a system. The various phases differ widely as far as needed information is concerned, so the precise manner in which a HIPO package is developed for a distinct phase is dependent upon the characteristics of that phase. The following three phases are sufficiently different to warrant special consideration:

1. The initial design phase.
2. Detail design phase.
3. Documentation and maintenance phase.

The *initial design phase* corresponds to the "conception" and "preliminary analysis" stages of the system development life cycle, given in Chapter 3. The *detail design phase* corresponds to the "system design" and "programming (implementation)" stages of the system development life cycle. The *documentation and maintenance phase* corresponds to the "system documentation, installation, and operation" stages of the system development life cycle.

The Initial Design Phase

The most fundamental version of a HIPO package is developed during the initial design phase and is called the *initial design package*. The initial design package is prepared by the design group and gives the overall design of the proposed or modified system. The overview diagrams are used by analysts to represent basic design features and the hierarchy diagram is used to show how the various functions fit together. The analyst's ideas go through design reviews until the desired level of functional capability is achieved; the final initial design package is then presented to management and other interested groups for comments and approval.

At the initial design level, the HIPO package is lacking in details necessary for implementation but adequately gives the scope of the project and can be used for scheduling and cost estimation. In this phase, the HIPO technique is used as a *design aid*.

The initial design phase may also require knowledge of the existing system and this is one area in which the HIPO technique achieves its greatest utility. Through the use of the hierarchy diagram in the visual table of contents and the overview diagrams of a HIPO package describing the existing system, an analyst or a representative of a sponsoring department can easily determine the functions performed by the existing system and can make evaluations and judgments accordingly.

Another consideration is that a system described through the use of the HIPO technique can be readily understood by a person who is not knowledgeable on the methods of implementation. This is precisely the case because HIPO is used to describe "what" a system does and not "how" the functions are performed.

The Detail Design Phase

During the detail design phase, the design and implementation groups complete the design of a system using the initial design package as a base. Usually, the implementation group adds the details necessary for implementation to the initial design package, and then uses the resulting design for implementation. In the computer field, implementation would normally take the form of computer programming. In other cases, implementation would involve the synthesis of system components, in whatever form that activity might take.

As the system is developed, the implementation group completes the HIPO package by filling in the extended description box and by adding to the initial design as deficiencies become evident during implementation. Frequently, systems do not function properly as they are designed and these deficiencies are uncovered only during the course of implementation. Thus, it is important that the implementation group go back to the design group for alterations to the "basic design"; this is the feedback cycle mentioned in Chapter 3. In the process of altering the basic design, the HIPO package must be continually updated to reflect changes to the functions performed by the system. Because a HIPO package shows function that is not completely dependent upon all of the details of implementation, it is not likely to require a significant number of modifications during system development.

The use of HIPO does not preclude the use of other descriptive techniques, such as flow charts and decision tables, and in fact, the implementation group may elect to use these techniques during development of the system. When additional techniques are used, they supplement the HIPO package and can be referenced in the extended description.

The document produced during the detail design phase is known as the *detail design package*. Since HIPO is used to aid in the implementation effort, it serves also as a *development tool* and presents an up-to-date description of the system as it is implemented.

The detail design package serves as excellent input to the documentation and maintenance phase, because it is easy to understand, complete, and accurate, and exists in a familiar form.

The Documentation and Maintenance Phase

The purpose of the documentation and maintenance phase is to prepare for operational use of the system and to record the design and implementation of the system for future modifications to the system and for subsequent development activity. The documents produced during this phase are referred to as *system documents*, which include the following:

1. Management overview of the new system.
2. Logic manuals that contain the technical information necessary for the maintenance process.
3. Reference manuals for users of the system.
4. Operator reference manuals that are used for the operation of data processing systems.

A HIPO package, by itself, does not constitute any of the system documents but serves as the primary input to the documentation and maintenance phase. The documents that most closely resemble the HIPO package are the logic manuals that are used for maintaining the system and for making changes to it. Logic manuals are developed to describe a system and are commonly known as the "documentation of the system."   In reality, however, effective documentation should include the four categories given above.

When HIPO is used as a design aid, development tool, and documentation technique, the design of a system and its documentation start out together and stay together during the system life cycle. The designer's ideas and the implementor's thoughts are recorded when they occur, through the use of HIPO, so much of the documentation is generated as a by-product of design and implementation.

The designer's ideas and implementor's thoughts are useful for the management overview as well as for familiarizing technical writers, who comprise the documentation and maintenance groups, with the scope of the project. The management overview is composed mainly of verbal descriptions, but the hierarchy diagram and high-level overview diagrams serve to depict the functions performed by the system in a meaningful fashion and to show the relationships between the various functional components. In cases where the hierarchy and overview diagrams contain excessive detailed information for the management overview, they may have to be redrawn eliminating some of the detail. Nevertheless, the HIPO technique does serve an important purpose in the managerial description.

The detail design package serves essentially as a set of logic manuals except that the diagrams are edited by the documentation group and references are made to flow charts, decision tables, and verbal descriptions that have been added to the detailed design package for clarification. It should be remembered that the detail design package is used for implementation and may be more detailed than necessary for maintenance and to educate new personnel. Normally, it is the lower-level detail diagrams that reflect implementation technique and conventions, and these diagrams are deleted when it is necessary to show logic but not show the details of computer programs. A useful aphorism is that, "the lower you go in the hierarchy diagram, the more the detail diagrams show implementation rather than function."

In the development of user and operator reference manuals, HIPO diagrams frequently serve their greatest utility by providing information to documentation personnel but do not constitute a significant portion of the manuals. HIPO diagrams do provide, however, an excellent means of presenting an overview of a system and serve an important purpose in introductory sections of user and operator reference manuals.

To sum up, the use of HIPO is a painless way of achieving effective design and documentation. Systems analysts and designers normally think in terms of the inputs and outputs of a system or program along with the processes involved. By requiring that designers and analysts record their thoughts, ideas, and concepts as HIPO diagrams, and by updating these diagrams through the various stages of design and implementation, documentation is achieved as a by-product of design and implementation and not as a separate and completely distinct step in the system life cycle. As a result, HIPO documentation is more accurate and tends to reflect meaningful subjects that are less vulnerable to change than is documentation that reflects solely the details of implementation.

ADVANTAGES OF USING HIPO

There is a natural tendency for a designer, analyst, or technical writer to ask why HIPO should be used at all, since systems have been designed, implemented, and documented for many years without it. Therefore, any systems or programming manager desiring to benefit his installation through the use of HIPO has a selling job to do. One of the best approaches is to point out the deficiencies in the present methods.

To begin with, conventional methods of design that employ flow charting techniques represent implementation-dependent thinking. Thus, designers and implementors can easily lose sight of the function of the system. As a result, functional interfaces are frequently "cloudy" because design and implementation activity exists at the unit level. Documentation is commonly disjointed because concepts are not tied together and the technical writer is called in after the system has been completed. Another consideration is that designers and implementors use different techniques, at differing levels of detail, to describe their work and this practice can play havoc with the managerial aspects of system development. Implementation-dependent techniques are also inefficient in the sense that it is difficult and time consuming to obtain information from a logic diagram—that is, unless you know what you are looking for in the first place. Other disadvantages are equally important but are not as obvious. The techniques used to design a system are often a hindrance to implementation personnel instead of an aid, and the current methodology does not have side benefits in the areas of management planning and education.

The advantages in using the HIPO technique are manifold and constitute a summarization of the ideas presented in this chapter. The major advantages are contained in the following list:

1. HIPO diagrams are similar in form, as are the various kinds of

HIPO packages.   Thus, the technique can be used by people with different operational needs.

2. HIPO permits a program or system to be easily understood because a familiar format is employed.

3. HIPO is a "thinking" aid as well as a design, development, and documentation tool.

4. A HIPO package provides a common visual base for education and communication.

5. The use of HIPO promotes efficiency because there is less duplication of information and effort, and more information can be obtained at a glance from a HIPO diagram than from the use of other descriptive techniques.

6. Because a HIPO package is intended to show function, it is not vulnerable to changes inherent in the implementation effort.

7. The HIPO technique is a means of capturing the thoughts of system designers and allows design and documentation to start out together in the system development life cycle.

8. The use of HIPO facilitates maintenance and testing because a clear definition of functional interfaces is provided, and because errors can be detected and isolated on a functional basis.

9. HIPO is a management tool because the functional approach allows planning and scheduling to be made accurately and early in the system development life cycle and because it provides a means of monitoring the development effort.

10. Documentation becomes a by-product of design, development, and testing because a set of HIPO packages is excellent source material for the documentation group.

The major advantage of HIPO, however, has not been stated but is implied by the above list; it is that the value of HIPO depends upon how it is used.   To a system's designer, it is a design aid.   To the implementation group, it is a development aid.   To the documentation group, it is a documentation tool.

DESIGN AND DOCUMENTATION AIDS

HIPO diagrams can and are frequently drawn with a pencil and paper—without any drawing aids.   In fact, it is commonplace for a

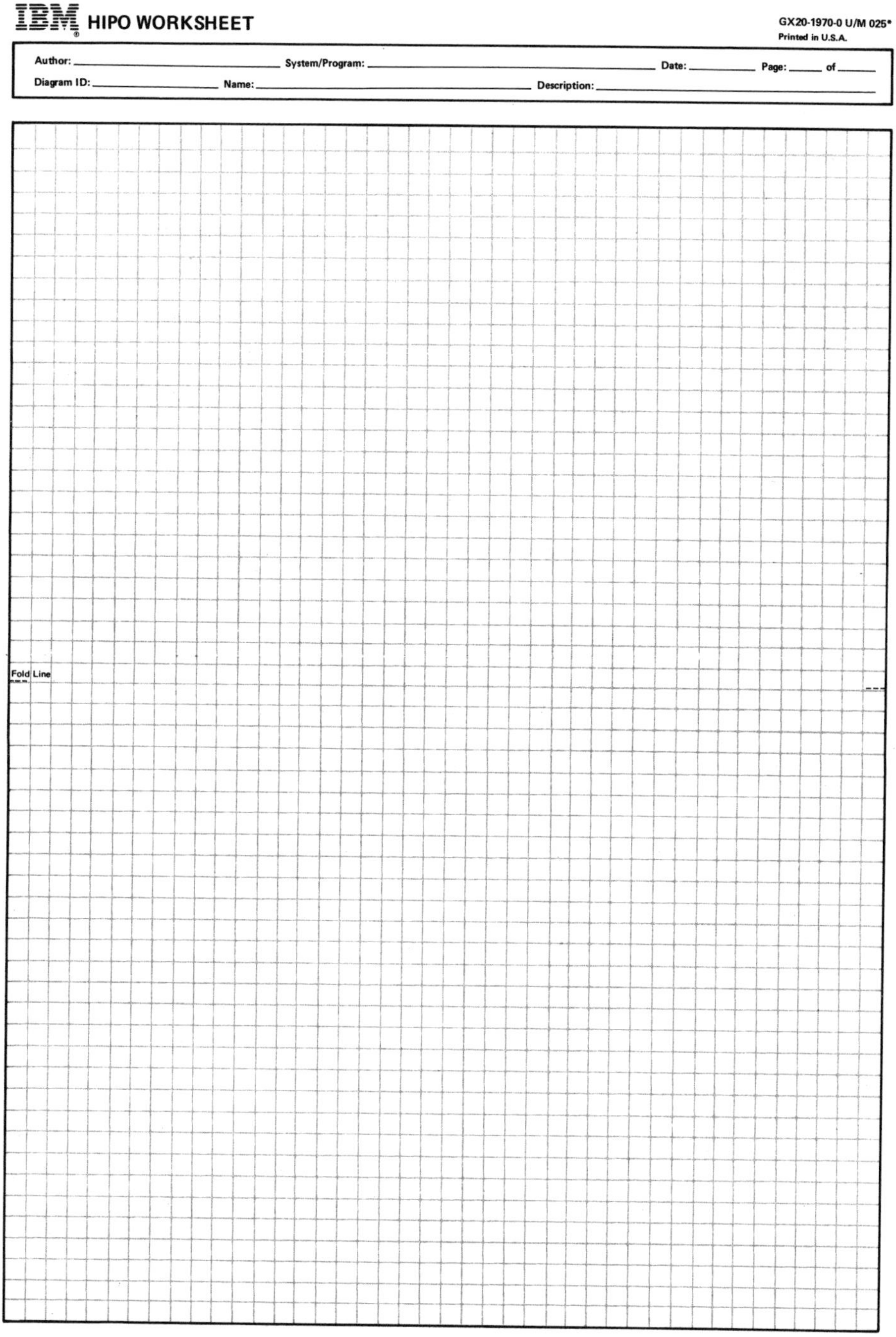

IBM HIPO WORKSHEET

GX20-1970-0 U/M 025*
Printed in U.S.A.

Author: ______ System/Program: ______ Date: ______ Page: ____ of ____

Diagram ID: ______ Name: ______ Description: ______

Fold Line

Figure 4.9 HIPO worksheet. (Used for hierarchy diagram and the legend.) (*Courtesy of IBM Corporation*)

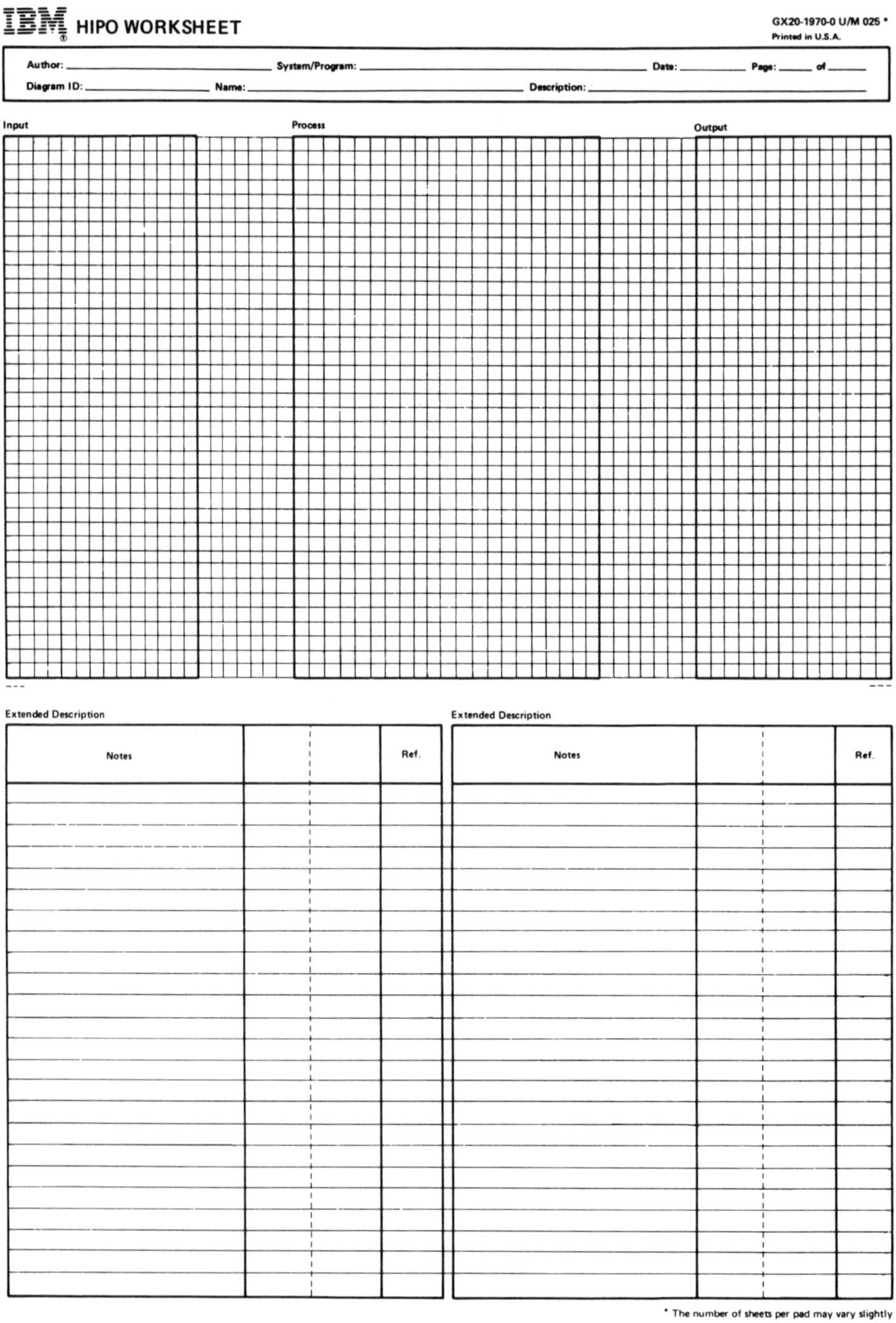

Figure 4.10 HIPO worksheet. (Used for overview and detail diagrams and the extended description.) (*Courtesy of IBM Corporation*)

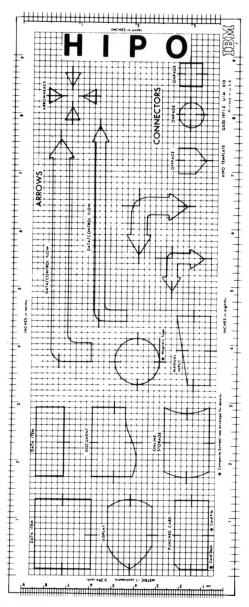

Figure 4.11 HIPO diagramming template. (*Courtesy of IBM Corporation*)

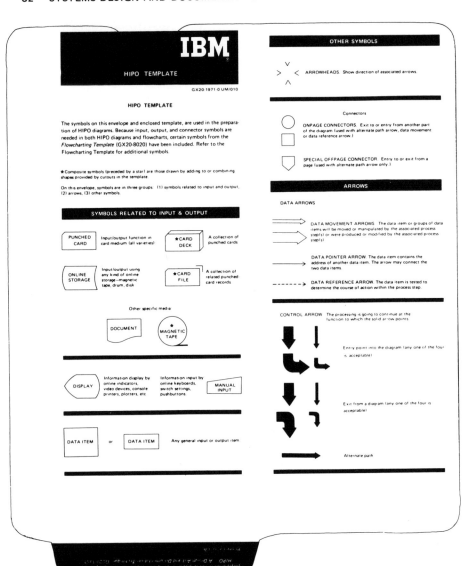

Figure 4.12 Jacket to the HIPO diagramming template giving the meaning of the various HIPO symbols. (*Courtesy of IBM Corporation*)

designer to "scratch out" a cryptic form of a HIPO diagram to record his ideas. When a system design is formalized, however, diagrams should be drawn using common graphic conventions.

Figures 4.9 and 4.10 depict typical HIPO worksheets, used for hierarchy diagrams, input-process-output diagrams, and extended descriptions. Figure 4.9 shows one side of the worksheet including areas for the input-process-output diagrams and the extended description. Figure 4.10 gives the flip side of the same worksheet; it is used for drawing the hierarchy diagram.

The symbols used in a HIPO package are relatively stable, even though some evolutionary changes will probably take place and that is why the legend is recommended in the visual table of contents. A HIPO diagramming template has been developed and is depicted in Figure 4.11. The meaning of the various symbols is given in Figure 4.12, the HIPO template jacket. The precise manner in which the various symbols are used is given in Chapter 7, "HIPO Conventions."

REFERENCES

HIPO–A Design Aid and Documentation Technique, White Plains, N.Y., IBM Corporation, 1974, Form GC20-1851.

HIPO: Design Aid and Documentation Tool, Poughkeepsie, N.Y., IBM Corporation, 1973, Form SR20-9413.

5 | SALES/ INVENTORY SYSTEM CASE STUDY

INTRODUCTION

One of the most common applications of computer technology is the *sales/inventory system* that provides the following services to an enterprise:

1. Maintains an updated inventory file.
2. Validates customer orders.
3. Prepares a sales report.
4. Prepares a daily inventory report.
5. Produces shipping orders and packing slips.
6. Generates customer billing invoices and an accounts receivable file.
7. Guarantees a specified inventory level by ordering inventory items when the quantity on hand is less than a threshold value and when current inventory is insufficient to satisfy an order (i.e., a back order).

The application is given as an example because most people are familiar with it and because the system is generally considered to be complicated due to the processing details involved but straightforward enough to be used as an example. The objective here is to give a HIPO description of a hypothetical system of this type and compare it, to a limited degree, with conventional techniques for describing systems.

CONVENTIONAL METHODS

Conventional methods for describing systems include flow charts, decision tables, and prose descriptions. The flow chart is the most widely used method and comes in two variations: program flow charts and system flow charts. The two types of flow charts are used here to describe the sales/inventory system and to illustrate the use of flow-charting methods.

Program Flow Chart

A *program flow chart* is generally considered to be a detailed description of the steps involved in the execution of a computer program or a procedural description of the operation of a system. The program or system is organized into meaningful segments, and the flow chart for a segment tells how that segment works.

Figure 5.1 gives a program flow chart for an initial phase of a sales/inventory system. In that phase, a transaction record representing a sales order is analyzed to insure that all of the necessary information is present on the input medium and that the information is valid. The program segment* is designed to write the transaction records to an intermediate file and then sort that file by inventory item number giving a transaction file. A tacit assumption is made that the sales/inventory system is run on the computer on a daily basis. Therefore, the output of the analysis-validation segment serves as input to the next segment that generates a daily sales report.

It is evident from Figure 5.1 that the program flow chart involves implementation-dependent thinking. It is also difficult to determine what the segment does from the flow chart because "you can't see the *forest* for the *trees*." In short, the program flow chart tells how a procedure is performed but is deficient in telling what the procedure is.   Becuase a program flow chart does involve implementation-dependent thinking, however, it would be a useful adjunct to a detail diagram.

*The term "routine" would be a suitable synonym for program segment, in this case.

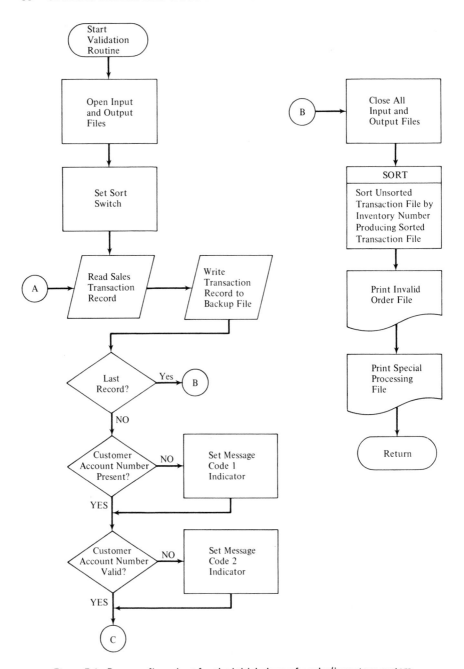

Figure 5.1 Program flow chart for the initial phase of a sales/inventory system.

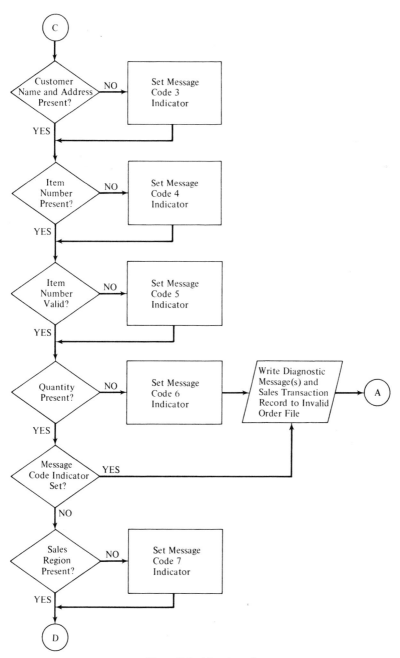

Figure 5.1   (*Continued*)

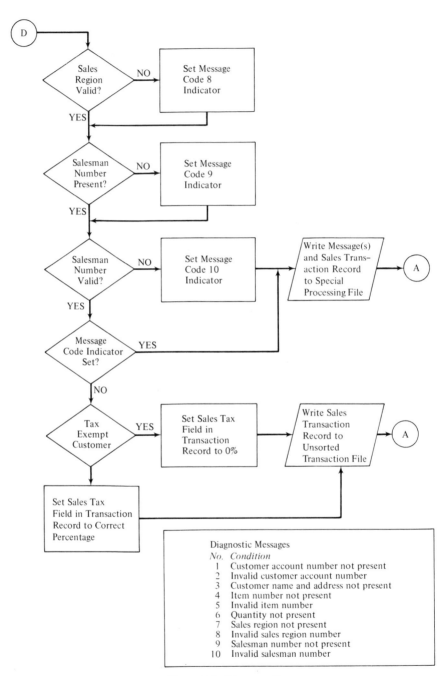

Figure 5.1 *(Continued)*

System Flow Chart

A *system flow chart* is generically considered to be an input-output diagram of a system. The operation of the system is divided into distinct phases and the inputs and outputs of each phase are depicted in symbolic form.

Figure 5.2 gives a system flow chart for the sales/inventory system. The diagram is useful for the operations group because it is possible to tell the exact nature of the inputs and outputs at a glance. Outputs from one phase of the system that serve as input to the next phase are readily apparent from the description; for example, the transaction file produced during the first phase, which prepares the inventory transaction, is used during the second phase, which processes the inventory transaction.

It is evident from Figure 5.2 that the system flow chart gives only the inputs and outputs of a system. Again, it is difficult to determine what the system does from the flow chart, since there is no indication of the processing that is performed.

Analysis

In spite of their widespread utilization, program and system flow charts are notably inadequate for systems design and evaluation. A program flow chart is too detailed and dependent upon implementation. A system flow chart is too general and does not provide the minimal capability for describing either *what* is being done or *how* it is being done.

A HIPO APPROACH

This section gives a HIPO package describing the sales/inventory system. It is recognized that the system, as a whole, is only partially described in the program and system flow charts of the previous section. However, this is the kind of situation that lends itself to a HIPO description, and the complete system is documented using the HIPO technique. A reader should be able to grasp the essence of the sales/inventory system easily from the HIPO package.

Visual Table of Contents

The visual table of contents of the HIPO package for the sales/inventory system is given in Figure 5.3. From the hierarchy dia-

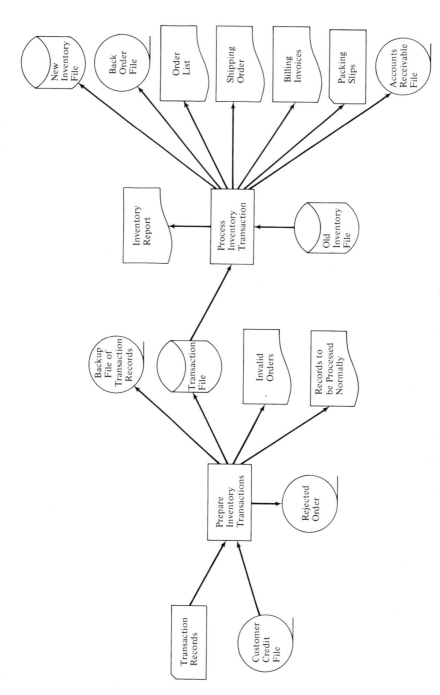

Figure 5.2   System flow chart of the sales/inventory system.

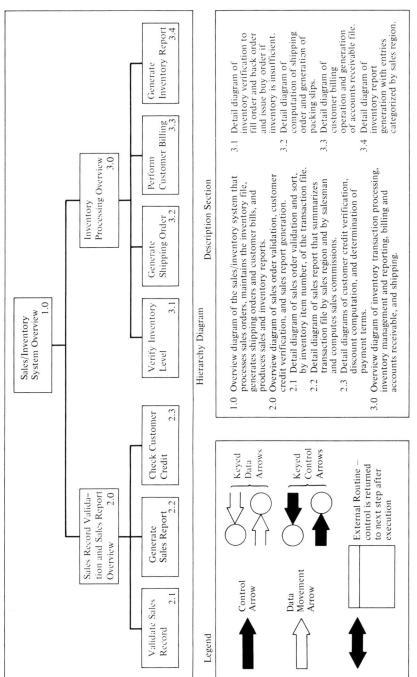

Figure 5.3 Visual table of contents of the HIPO package describing the sales/inventory system.

gram, it is evident that the system is subdivided into two functional components:

1. One that prepares sales/inventory transaction records for processing.
2. The other that processes the sales/inventory transaction records and generates associated files and reports.

This fact is evident from the second level (from the top) in the hierarchy diagram that contains two rectangular boxes, numbered 2.0 and 3.0. These boxes represent overview diagrams. The overview diagram of the complete system is given at the top level; it contains roughly the same amount of information as the system flow chart. The third (or bottom) level in the hierarchy diagram represents detail diagrams. The number of levels in the hierarchy diagram is arbitrary; however, a set of general guidelines for drawing HIPO diagrams is given in a later chapter. Also, the number of levels of overview diagrams and of detail diagrams is dependent upon the application. The top level is always an overview diagram; the bottom level is always a set of detail diagrams.

The legend indicates that the broad solid arrow denotes control flow and the broad open arrow denotes data movement. The external routine box attached to a broad solid double-headed arrow denotes the use of a routine or system external to the system being described. Other symbols are introduced later in the chapter.

The description section provides additional information about each box in the hierarchy diagram, without requiring that the reader go to an overview or detail diagram to find information on a particular function. Although the description section is optional, it serves an important purpose. When it is necessary to locate a specific function for maintenance or education purposes, that function can be located directly through the hierarchy diagram, eliminating a lengthy search through overview and detail diagrams, or without HIPO, through a myriad of system and program flow charts.

Overview Diagrams

In the example of a HIPO package for the sales/inventory system, there are two levels of overview diagrams: the top level and the second level. The top level consists of a single overview diagram, given as Figure 5.4, and labeled as 1.0 in the hierarchy diagram.

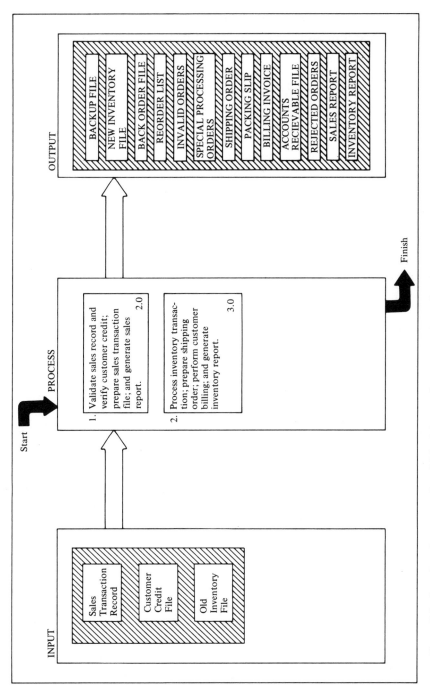

INPUT

- Sales Transaction Record
- Customer Credit File
- Old Inventory File

Start

PROCESS

1. Validate sales record and verify customer credit; prepare sales transaction file; and generate sales report. 2.0

2. Process inventory transaction; prepare shipping order; perform customer billing; and generate inventory report. 3.0

Finish

OUTPUT

- BACKUP FILE
- NEW INVENTORY FILE
- BACK ORDER FILE
- REORDER LIST
- INVALID ORDERS
- SPECIAL PROCESSING ORDERS
- SHIPPING ORDER
- PACKING SLIP
- BILLING INVOICE
- ACCOUNTS RECIEVABLE FILE
- REJECTED ORDERS
- SALES REPORT
- INVENTORY REPORT

Figure 5.4 Overview diagram numbered 1.0 of the sales/inventory system. (This is the highest-level diagram in the HIPO package.)

The inputs and outputs are identified but not associated with a particular subfunction or with a specific storage medium. The steps in the process block are enclosed in boxes to indicate that they correspond to subfunctions described by an overview or detail diagram. Each box, relating to a subfunction, contains a number in its lower right-hand corner that identifies the corresponding HIPO diagram.

The second-level overview diagrams are given in Figures 5.5 and 5.6; they are logical extensions to the highest-level diagram and possess a similar format. It should be noted that the inputs and outputs are also enclosed in a large box to indicate that they should be interpreted collectively. (The shading is optional and is used for emphasis.) Again, specific device and medium types are not shown. The question of the level at which to include device types is dependent upon the person developing the HIPO package and upon installation guidelines. The author prefers to leave the device type open until the detail diagram level is reached.

The reader will note that as we progress down through the hierarchy diagram, the diagrams become more specific about the functions that are performed, and that the output blocks and subsequent input blocks reflect intermediate records and files.

Detail Diagrams

The objective of a detail diagram is to relate specific functions to specific inputs and outputs. A detail diagram may optionally reflect specific device types.

The detail diagram numbered 2.1 corresponding to the "Validate sales transaction records and generate sorted transaction file" subfunction is given as Figure 5.7. Several new concepts are introduced: A series of steps to be repeated successively is enclosed in a box and identified with the keyword DO. In this example, the set of steps is executed for each sales transaction record. There is at least one other method or representing a repetitive procedure; it is given later in this chapter, and discussed more fully in Chapter 7, "HIPO Conventions." Detail diagram numbered 2.1 depicts the representation of the external routine SORT used to sort a data file. The double-ended control arrow attached to the external reference box indicates that control is returned to the calling program from the SORT

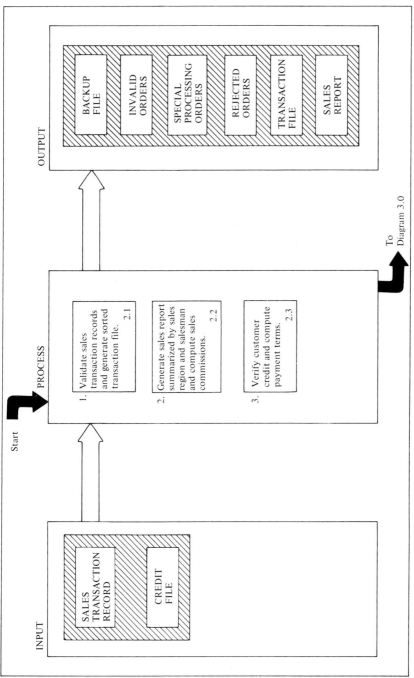

Figure 5.5 Overview diagram numbered 2.0 of the sales/inventory system. (This diagram corresponds to the "sales record validation and sales report" subfunction.)

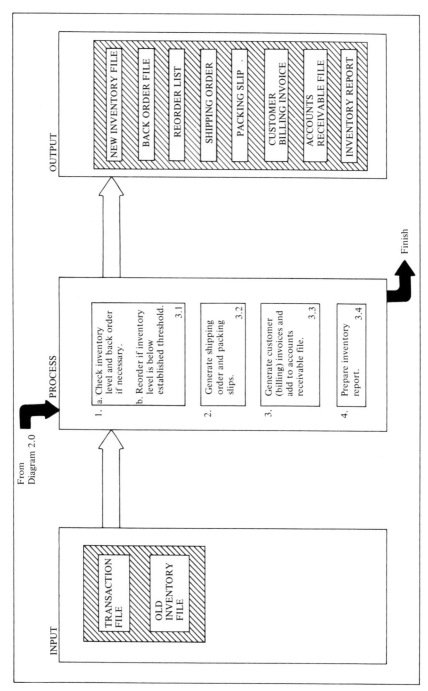

Figure 5.6 Overview diagram numbered 3.0 of the sales/inventory system. (This diagram corresponds to the "inventory processing" subfunction.)

routine.   The diagram also shows a keyed data movement arrow connector that is customarily used when the use of a data movement arrow alone would complicate the diagram unnecessarily.   (In this case, for example, the invalid order file, written in step 1.B(1), serves as input to step 3.) It should be noted that inputs and outputs relate to specific steps in the process and that specific types of storage devices and media are indicated.   As was mentioned earlier, the farther down the hierarchy diagram you go, the closer the diagram comes to representing implementation.

The detail diagram numbered 2.2 corresponding to the "generate sales report" subfunction is given as Figure 5.8.   The diagram illustrates two additional concepts: First, there is no formal means of representing a temporary file, so it is denoted in diagram 2.2 by an output symbol drawn with dashed lines.   Second, step numbered 2 is composed of two substeps that perform a related function and use the same input.   In this case, the substeps are enclosed in a box to indicate that they take a common input.   The extended description is omitted in this and in subsequent detail diagrams because no new concepts are introduced.

The detail diagram numbered 2.3 corresponding to the "verify customer credit" subfunction is given as Figure 5.9.   The diagram is intended to describe the case wherein for each transaction record that is read, the credit file is searched for that customer's credit record.   This technique is contrasted with the DO box that was used in Figure 5.7, which describes a similar procedure.   Since HIPO is intended to communicate, the technique should be selected that best communicates the required information for the case at hand.   It should also be noticed in Figure 5.9, that the transaction file appears as an input and as an output, which means the file is updated.   This is the standard convention for denoting a file, record, or field that serves as output as well as input.

The detail diagram numbered 3.1 corresponding to the "check inventory level" subfunction is given as Figure 5.10.   The diagram demonstrates the case where two input files serve as input to the same step; in this case, the files are sorted and a "match" is made between the transaction file and the old inventory file on the inventory item number.   The diagram additionally depicts two output data movement arrows from two distinct steps (i.e., steps lc and ld and also lc and le) that join a single output symbol.   This is termed

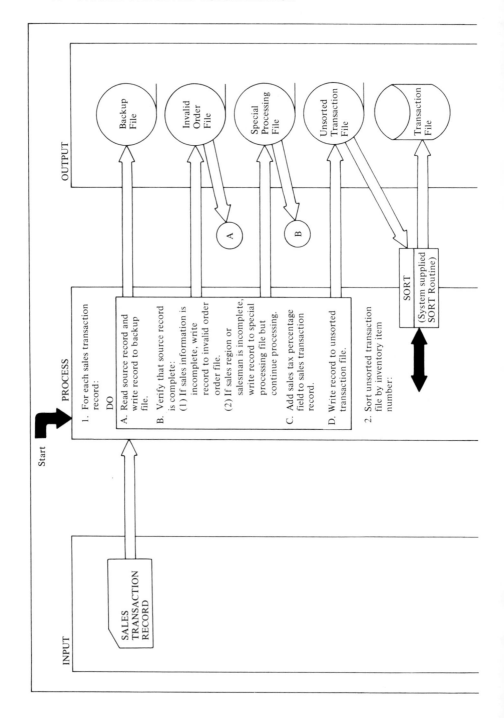

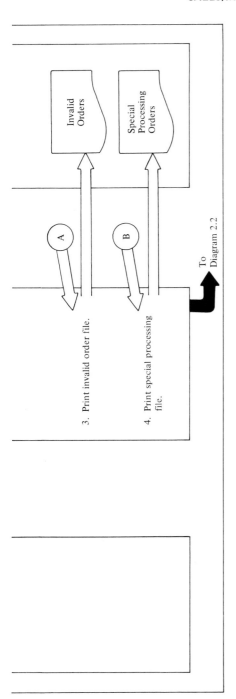

Notes	Routine	Label	Flow Chart	Ref.
1. Process sales transaction records, validating various fields, and producing a backup file, invalid order file, special processing file, and unsorted transaction file.	INVALID	BEGIN	VAL1	2.1.1
2. Sort unsorted transaction file producing transaction file. Use system sort routine.	INVALID	SORT	—	2.1.2
3. Print invalid order file.	INVALID	P1	VAL2	2.1.3
4. Print special processing file.	INVALID	P2	VAL2	2.1.4

Extended Description

Figure 5.7 Detail diagram numbered 2.1 of the sales/inventory system. (This diagram corresponds to the "validate sales transaction records and generate sorted transaction file" subfunction.)

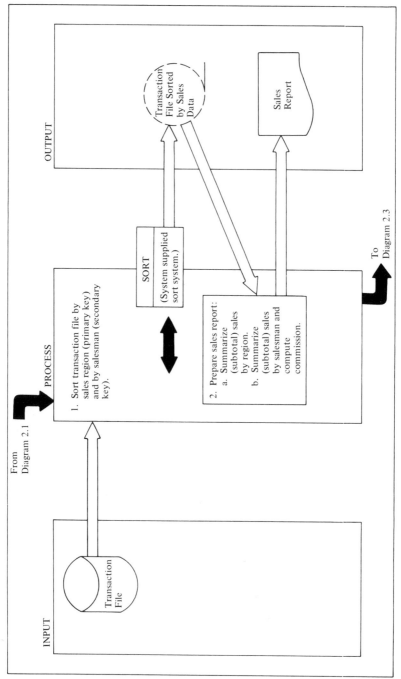

Figure 5.8   Detail diagram numbered 2.2 of the sales/inventory system with extended description omitted.   (This diagram corresponds to the "generate sales report" subfunction.)

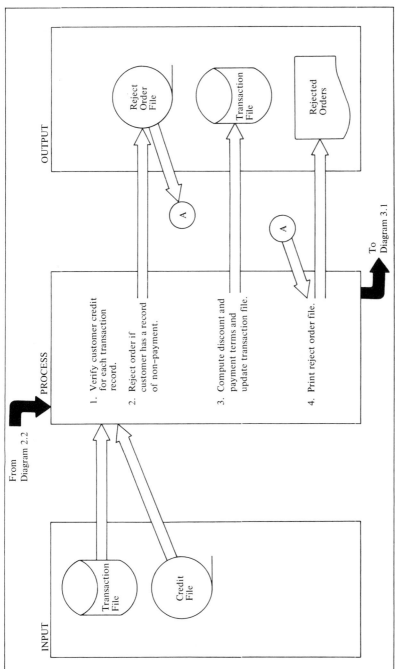

Figure 5.9 Detail diagram numbered 2.3 of the sales/inventory system with extended description omitted. (This diagram corresponds to the "verify customer credit" subfunction.)

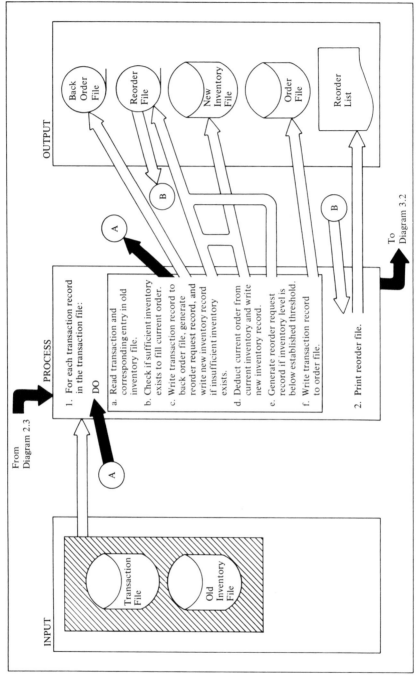

Figure 5.10 Detail diagram numbered 3.1 of the sales/inventory system with extended description omitted. (This diagram corresponds to the "check inventory level" subfunction.)

a *multiple output arrow*, which simply denotes that two or more steps provide output to the same output entry. Diagram numbered 3.1 also depicts a keyed control arrow connector that indicates that control is passed between the specified steps. (In this case, step 1c passes control to step 1a.)

Detail diagrams numbered 3.2, 3.3, and 3.4, which complete the HIPO package, are given as Figures 5.11, 5.12, and 5.13, respectively. The diagrams further demonstrate how the concepts introduced earlier can be used. Diagram 3.4, shown in Figure 5.13, demonstrates a *multiple input arrow* indicating that the same input entry is used as input to two or more steps.

A Brief Note

The HIPO package given in this section is intended solely to demonstrate the concepts introduced in the preceding chapter. There is no right way or wrong way to use HIPO. This is so because HIPO is a set of conventions for describing systems and the degree to which the conventions are adopted is based on personal preference and installation standards.

COMMENTARY ON THE USE OF HIPO

There is a natural tendency to regard HIPO as a replacement for flow charts, decision tables, and so forth. This is definitely not the case. The use of HIPO provides a level of system description that is impossible with the older techniques. In short, HIPO does not replace the other techniques; it simply provides a means of presenting the kind of information that would be cumbersome to present with those techniques. Through the extended description, HIPO can point to the various other descriptive techniques.

Another consideration is that the development of a HIPO package— even a thorough and complete HIPO package—does not automatically fulfill the documentation requirement. The use of HIPO is only a means of achieving good documentation, and the form of documentation that is most closely related to a HIPO package is the logic manual.

When a system is designed and documented using HIPO, the fact that function is described is significant. This is the case because the system will perform those functions it was intended to perform and

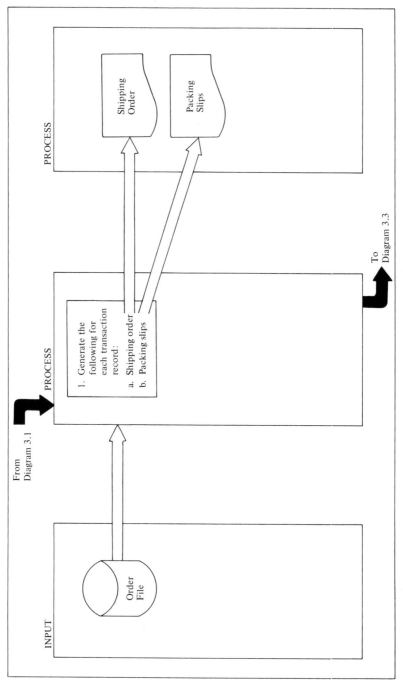

Figure 5.11 Detail diagram numbered 3.2 of the sales/inventory system with extended description omitted. (This diagram corresponds to the "generate shipping order and packing slips" subfunction.)

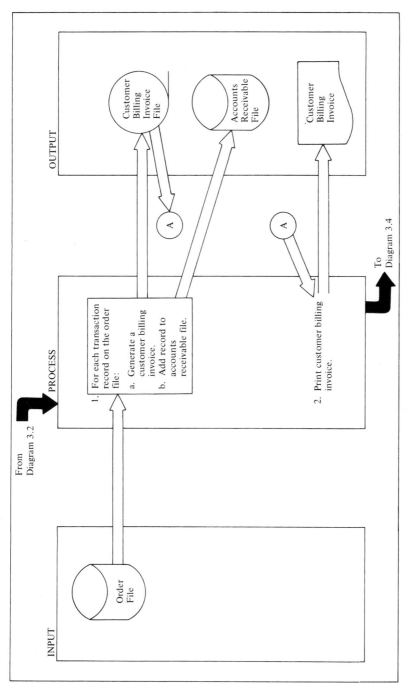

Figure 5.12 Detail diagram numbered 3.3 of the sales/inventory system with extended description omitted. (This diagram corresponds to the "generate customer invoices . . ." subfunction.)

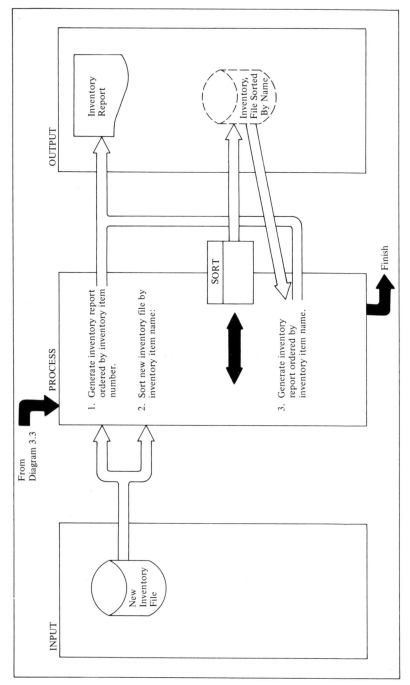

Figure 5.13   Detail diagram numbered 3.4 of the sales/inventory system with extended description omitted.   (This diagram corresponds to the "prepare inventory report" subfunction.)

thereby satisfy user requirements. *With HIPO, structure must always follow function.*

REFERENCES

HIPO—A Design Aid and Documentation Technique, White Plains, New York, IBM Corporation, 1974, Form GC20-1851.

Katzan, H., *Introduction to Computer Science*, New York, Petrocelli/Charter Publishers, 1975.

6

HIPO
DIAGRAMMING

INTRODUCTION

Most people would regard systems design and documentation as an art, and the use of HIPO could also be placed into that category. HIPO is a visual technique and because of that fact, the effectiveness of a HIPO diagram is dependent upon the use of distinctive symbols and visual indicators in a meaningful context. The objective of this chapter is to give a general idea of how a HIPO package is created.

BASIC CONSIDERATIONS

The development of an effective HIPO package is based on four simple concepts: iterative refinement, boxes, arrows, and keys. These concepts are used in all types of HIPO packages.

Iterative Refinement

The design of an effective system is a complex process. At least two considerations are involved. First, the designer does not simply "dash out" a complete design with or without the use of HIPO. Effective designs evolve as they are affected by design reviews, changing

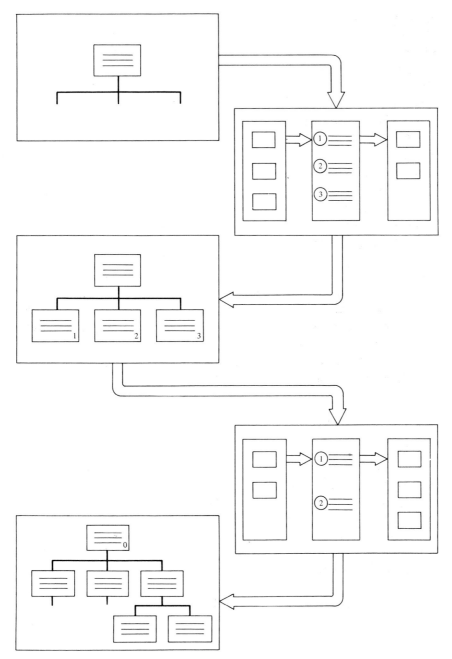

Figure 6.1 The use of iterative refinement to construct hierarchy, overview, and detail diagrams.

requirements, development of new methodology, and the matura-
tion of the designer's original ideas. Secondly, the task of breaking
out function by level of detail is not as straightforward as one might
imagine. The process of reworking a HIPO package or the diagrams
of a package to achieve a satisfactory design is referred to as *iterative
refinement.*

At the package level, iterative refinement simply refers to the rework of a HIPO package resulting from design reviews, changing
requirements, and new methodology. This is a natural process that
may be both progressive and regressive, depending upon the validity
of the feedback process causing the changes in system requirements.

At the diagram level, iterative refinement refers to the iterative
process of using the hierarchy diagram to develop overview diagrams
and of using overview diagrams to help develop the next level in the
hierarchy diagram, as shown in Figure 6.1. In the example, the basic
functional description of the system, corresponding to the top-level
box in the hierarchy diagram, is used to construct the corresponding
overview diagram. The steps in the process block of the overview
diagram are used to develop the next lower level in the hierarchy
diagram, and so forth.

Additional insight into the development of hierarchy, overview,
and detail diagrams is given later in the chapter.

Boxes

In spite of its obvious simplicity, the box is used to group entries
that are physically or logically related. The concept not only applies
to the input entries, the output entries, and the steps in the process
block, but also to the grouping of entries within these major components of an overview or detail diagram. The use of boxes for grouping
is suggested in Figure 6.2; the concept is also used in previous
examples.

The use of boxes has a visual advantage because the human eye
normally groups entries enclosed in a box and this fact helps in the
communication process. When it is desired to attract the reader's
attention to a particular set of entries, shading can be used, as demonstrated in Figure 6.2 and in the previous chapter.

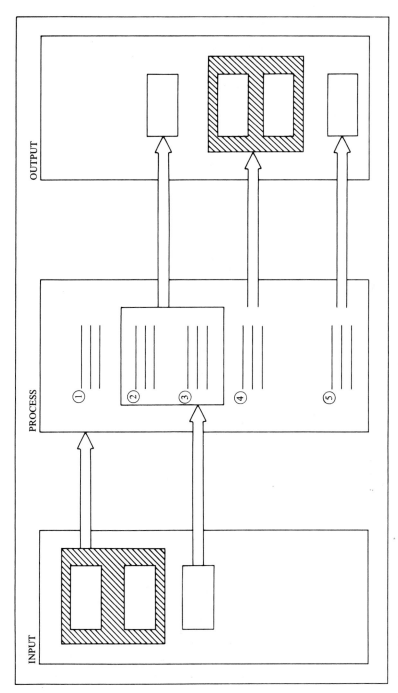

Figure 6.2   The box is used to group entries with a physical or logical relationship.   Shading can be used to attract the reader's attention to a particular set of entries.

Arrows

The *arrow* is a visual indicator of movement and leads the eye from one place on a chart to another. Thus far, clear wide arrows have been used to show data movement and solid wide arrows have been used to show control flow. Two other uses of the arrow are recognized:

1. The solid line arrow is used to show a pointer to a data element; and
2. The dashed line arrow is used to represent data reference, as in the case where a data value is tested in a conditional operation.

Figure 6.3 gives an idea of how solid and dashed line arrows might be used. The input box in Figure 6.3 suggests that the inputs and outputs to a process are not restricted to files and records. *Inputs and outputs can take any form and are limited only by the system being designed or documented.* In Figure 6.3, the input takes the form of registers and data areas.* In a noncomputer application, inputs and outputs could take the form of a verbal response, a slip of paper, a visual indicator, or any other form of human communication.

Keys

A *key* is a distinctive symbol used for identification. In HIPO diagramming, a key is most frequently used to point to an entry or to establish a relationship between two entries. Both cases are demonstrated in Figure 6.4, in which a key is represented by a digit or letter enclosed in a small circle.

An example of a key used to establish a relationship between two entries is shown in the process block and the extended description, in which the number determines the correspondence between a step in the process block and a line in the extended description. The enclosing circles are sometimes omitted in this case.

An example of a key used to point to an entry is shown in the output block where the output of one step serves as input to another step and a continuous arrow would not be appropriate.

The practice of using a key together with an arrow occurs frequently and the construct is called a *directional key* (Figure 6.5).

*Data areas are frequently referred to as control blocks in systems programming.

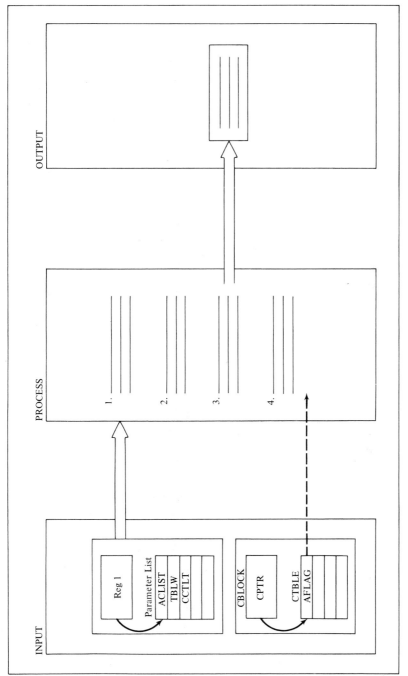

Figure 6.3 Portion of a HIPO diagram showing the use of the solid line arrow to represent a data pointer and a dashed line arrow to represent a data reference.

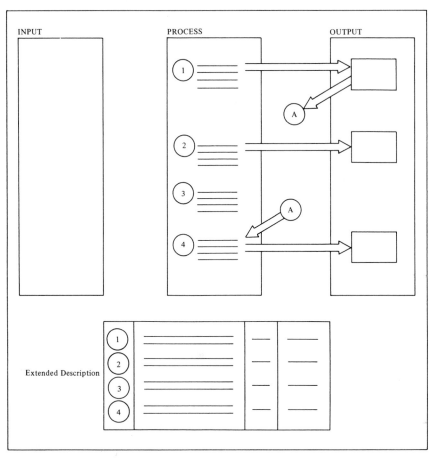

INPUT   PROCESS   OUTPUT

Extended Description

Figure 6.4 The key is used in HIPO to point to an entry or to establish a relationship.

The major advantage of the use of a directional key is that it helps to make a diagram less complex and easier to read and understand.

DEVELOPMENT OF THE VISUAL TABLE OF CONTENTS

The visual table of contents serves as an organization chart of a system or program. Its major component, the hierarchy diagram, can be developed concurrently with the first few levels of overview diagrams, as suggested earlier in this chapter as an example of iterative refinement, or it can be developed as a top-down plan. In either case, the hierarchy diagram is usually adjusted considerably during the design and development of the project.

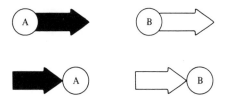

Figure 6.5 The arrow used in combination with a key is called a *directional key.*

Hierarchy Diagram

The single box at the top level of the hierarchy diagram serves as a statement of the overall function of the system or program. Successive levels in the hierarchy diagram subdivide the overall function into subjunctions, sub-subfunctions, etc. Each box in the hierarchy diagram corresponds to an overview diagram or to a detail diagram.

The hierarchy diagram serves several purposes. Initially, the hierarchy diagram is used as a design tool and is used to define a system functionally; once the system is developed, the hierarchy diagram serves as a directory that tells where a specific function is described by an overview or detail diagram. The hierarchy diagram is also used as a scheduiling and planning tool for large systems development. In this case, it may be desirable to develop a hierarchy of hierarchy diagrams. The design group may specify the overall structure of a system on a functional basis and turn each subfunction over to a development group for follow-on design and implementation. Thus, we may have an overall system plan and a set of development plans, as suggested in Figure 6.6. Each development group may wish to structure its work in a similar manner resulting in a hierarchy of system plans. This option is suggested in Figure 6.7.

Size of the Hierarchy Diagram

The size of the hierarchy diagram is frequently of concern and a good practice is to limit its size to one page, so that needed information can be located easily. For large systems, the one-page limit necessitates a hierarchy of diagrams that lends itself to effective scheduling and planning.

Dashed-Line Boxes

Because a HIPO package represents function and not structure and implementation, it is necessary to have the capability of denoting

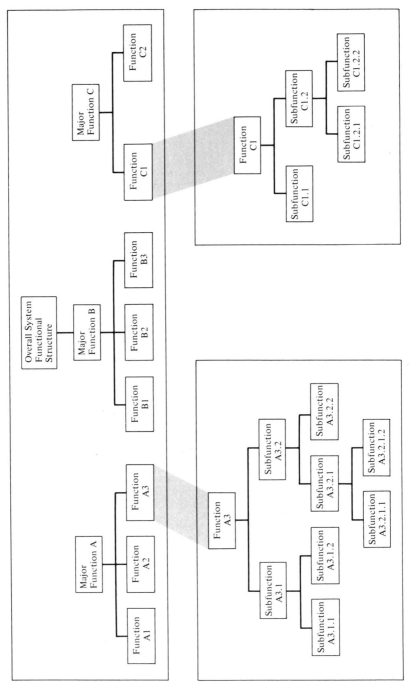

Figure 6.6 The hierarchy diagram can be used as a scheduling and planning tool by structuring the system on a top-down basis.

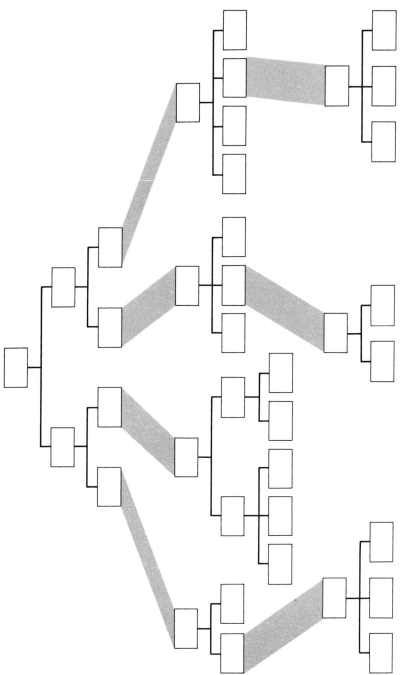

Figure 6.7 A system can be structured as a hierarchy of plans.

special conditions in a hierarchy diagram such as the following:

1. Functions performed by other systems.
2. Functions that have been defined but not supported by over-view and detail diagrams.

In general, any method of representation is satisfactory; however, a dashed-line box has been used for both cases, as shown in Figure 6.8. The precise meaning of a dashed-line box, or any other symbol as a matter of fact, should be given in the legend.

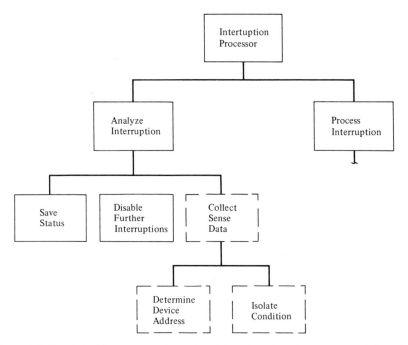

Figure 6.8 The dashed-line box can be used to denote functions that have been defined but not yet represented by overview or detail diagrams.

Legend and Description Sections

The development of the legend and the optional description section are usually governed by installation guidelines. The legend normally accompanies the hierarchy diagram in the initial design package—although the legend can justifiably be omitted until the documentation phase of the system life cycle.

The need for a description section is determined by the amount of information that is placed in each box in the hierarchy diagram. If the entries in the hierarchy diagram contain only names of functions, then the only way for a reader to obtain definitive information on a function is to consult the description section or go to the overview and detail diagrams. Since obtaining a general statement of a function from its overview or detail diagram is inconvenient, at best, the use of the description section is preferable—at all stages of system development.

DEVELOPMENT OF OVERVIEW AND DETAIL DIAGRAMS

Because of their graphical similarity, overview and detail diagrams are developed in a similar manner. Both types of diagrams use input, process, and output blocks and involve the systematic specification of outputs, processes, and inputs.

Specification of Outputs

The first step in creating an input-process-output diagram is to list the outputs of the function. Listing of the outputs prior to developing the steps of the process and the inputs is preferred to concurrent development because the needed outputs of a function are generally known beforehand. If the topmost overview diagram of a system is being developed, then the outputs can be taken from the system requirements.

Some analysts prefer to develop the process block first or to develop the three blocks concurrently; however, this is a doubtful strategy. The effectiveness of a system, program, or function is determined by its outputs—otherwise, why have the system, program, or function in the first place? Thus, it would seem prudent to list the outputs first.

Specification of Inputs and Processes

The input and process blocks can be filled in separately or concurrently. The input entries should be listed and placed in the input block. The steps that comprise the function should be placed in the process block; the description of each step should be as concise as possible, since each normally corresponds to a lower-level diagram. Abbreviations should not be used. During the specification of the input and process blocks, the intermediate output* of one step that serves as input to a subsequent step in that process may also be identified and added to the output block.   Some fairly obvious considerations apply to the process block:

1. If there is nothing to say in a process block or it is impossible to identify more than one step, then the analyst has gone too far in subdividing the function and should back up one level.
2. If an input or output entry is required that is not specified in a higher-level diagram, then the higher-level diagram is not developed correctly. (Intermediate output is excluded.) Similarly, if a low-level function is needed and not specified or implied in a higher-level diagram, then the higher-level diagram should be reworked.

The next step is to connect the input, process, and output blocks in a meaningful manner. The connection is made differently for overview and detail diagrams.

Completion of an Overview Diagram

Completion of an overview diagram is straightforward; the input block is connected to the process block with one data movement arrow and the process block is connected to the output block with one data movement arrow. At this stage in system or program development, the input and output entries are not associated with specific steps in the process block.

Input and output entries in an overview diagram are normally represented by small rectangular boxes. This is satisfactory at the overview level, because it is not necessary to associate an input or output with a specific device or medium.

Completion of a Detail Diagram.

In a detail diagram, it is necessary to associate input and output entries with specific steps in the process block. Initially this is done with single arrows, as shown in Figure 6.9. At this state, it is important to "get the details down," and overall appearance is secondary. The originator of the diagram is the only person who is going to see

---

*Intermediate output is defined as output of a process that serves as input to the same process, but which is not included in the input block of a diagram at the same level or as output of a block at a higher level.

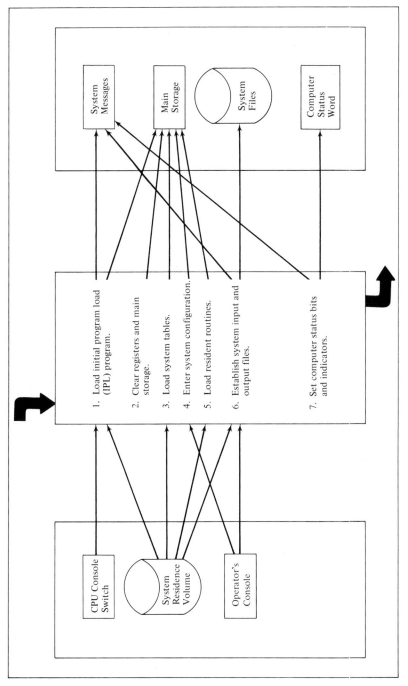

Figure 6.9 Preliminary detail diagram for an initial program load (IPL) routine for an operating system.

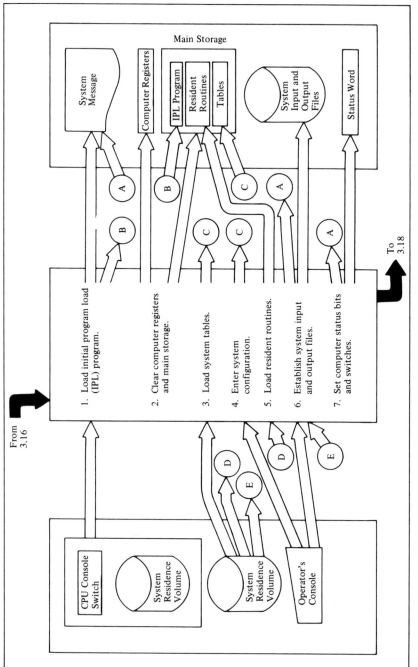

Figure 6.10 Polished version of the detail diagram of Figure 6.9 describing an initial program load (IPL) routine. (Extended description is omitted.)

or use it.   An input or output entry may be represented by any symbol, such as a simple box, since information is more important than adherence to an installation's diagramming conventions.

The next step is to rework and edit the diagram so that it communicates visually and is technically accurate.   At *this* stage, the installation's diagramming conventions should be used.   Appropriate input and output symbols should be selected to represent actual devices and media, and the extended description should be constructed for implementation packages.

A polished version of the initial program load (IPL) routine, given in roughly drawn form in Figure 6.9, is given in Figure 6.10.   Some of the concepts covered earlier in the chapter are depicted in Figure 6.10.   In the input box, the CPU console switch and the system residence volume that are used to perform a bootstrap load of the system are enclosed in a box for grouping since the devices function together during IPL.   Keys are used for clarity and the stages in the process block are stated as briefly as possible.

Remarks on the Detail Diagram

Detail diagrams can vary widely in the amount of detail they represent.   The detail diagrams in this book would probably be considered "high-level" detail diagrams, which means they do not contain a large amount of detail.   In actual practice, detail diagrams go down to the bit, byte, or word level in describing various types of system and application programs.

The flexibility in diagramming capability is one of the major advantages of using the HIPO technique.   A system or program can always be described at a level of detail that is appropriate to the system being described.

REFERENCES

HIPO—A design Aid and Documentation Technique, White Plains, New York, IBM Corporation, 1974, Form GC20-1851.

HIPO: Design Aid and Documentation Tool, Poughkeepsie, New York, IBM Corporation, 1973, Form SR20-9413.

Katzan, H., *Operating Systems: A Pragmatic Approach*, New York, Van Nostrand Reinhold Company, 1973.

OS/VS1 IPL and NIP Logic, Endicott, New York, IBM Corporation, 1973, Form SY24-5160.

7 | HIPO CONVENTIONS

INTRODUCTION

A system's group, a designer, an analyst, or a programmer electing to use HIPO would normally adopt a set of diagramming conventions to insure consistency between HIPO packages developed by different people, and among the diagrams in a single HIPO package. While the "Hierarchy, *plus* Input, Process, Output" concept is well defined, the specific conventions for drawing HIPO diagrams are not and can vary between installations. The objective of this chapter is to establish diagramming conventions that can be used as a standard. Most concepts covered in this chapter have been presented earlier in a different context or have been used in appropriate examples.

GENERAL DIAGRAMMING CONVENTIONS

Communication among humans implies a set of operational conventions that are pretty much taken for granted; conventions in this class are rarely stated because they are usually considered to be obvious. A few HIPO conventions of this sort are given in this section.

Arrows are drawn primarily from left to right and from top to bottom and are placed adjacent to the entries involved. The use of the various types* of arrows must always be consistent with the definition given in the legend, and the origin and destination of an arrow must always be clear. The latter point is demonstrated in Figure 7.1. Another useful, and perhaps necessary, convention is that the box should be used *only* to group functionally related entries and that abbreviations within boxes should not be used.

The width of an arrow is not significant, as long as the distinction between a wide arrow, denoting control of data movement, and a line arrow, denoting either a pointer or data reference, is maintained. Normally, however, a wider arrow is used with overview diagrams than with detail diagrams, as shown in Figure 7.2

VISUAL TABLE OF CONTENTS

The *visual table of contents* serves as a directory to a HIPO package and must be the first section of the package. When HIPO is used as a documentation technique, the visual table of contents is normally preceded by a short description of how the HIPO package can be used to obtain information about an existing or proposed system.

Hierarchy Diagram

The *hierarchy diagram* is a required entry in the visual table of contents and gives the functional structure of a program or system. Overview diagrams appear at higher levels in the hierarchy diagram; detail diagrams appear at lower levels in the hierarchy diagram. Obviously, the amount of detail in overview diagrams can vary and the amount of detail in detail diagrams can also vary. Therefore, it is necessary to establish an operational convention here. It is simply that *the level of detail should increase for each level in the hierarchy diagram as one goes from top to bottom.*

Each box in the hierarchy diagram should have an identification number that refers to the overview or detail diagram corresponding to that function. For simple diagrams, the boxes can be numbered sequentially as shown in Figure 7.3. When changes must be made to the underlying functional structure, the diagram can be renumbered.

Hierarchy diagrams corresponding to complex systems or systems for which modifications are expected should be numbered in a

---

*The types of arrows given in Chapter 6 are: data movement, control flow, data pointer, and data reference.

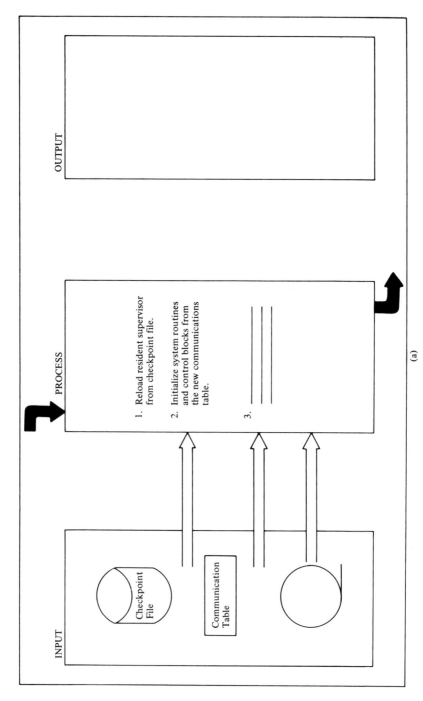

Figure 7.1   The origin and destination of an arrow must always be clear.   (a) Unclear and possibly misleading.   (Continued on next page.)

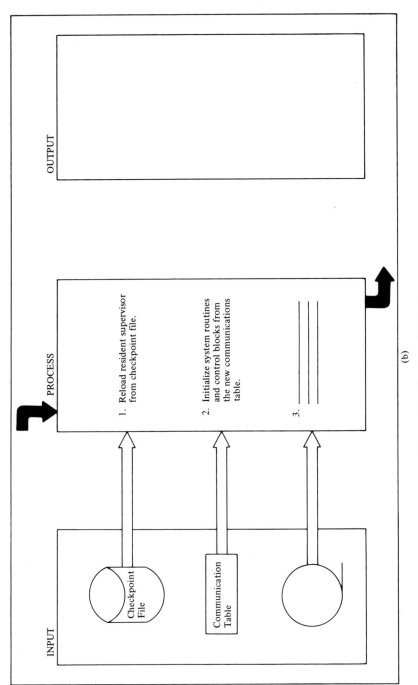

PROCESS

1. Reload resident supervisor from checkpoint file.

2. Initialize system routines and control blocks from the new communications table.

3.

INPUT

Checkpoint File

Communication Table

(b)

Figure 7.1 (*Continued*) (b) Satisfactory.

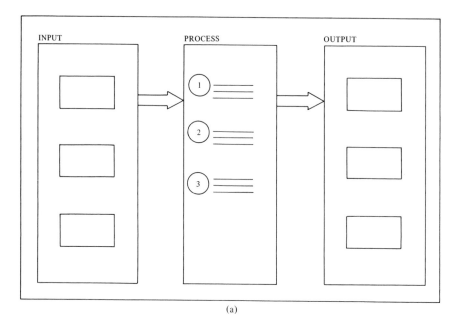

(a)

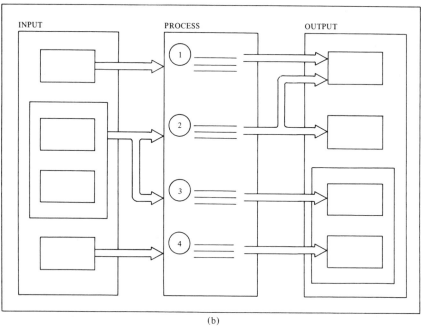

(b)

Figure 7.2   A wider arrow, normally, is used with overview diagrams (a) than with detail
diagrams (b).

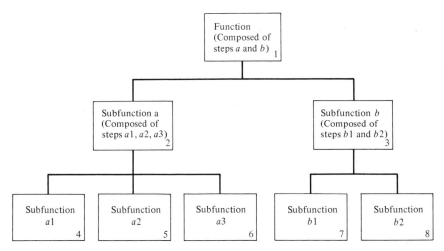

Figure 7.3 In simple hierarchy diagrams, the boxes can be numbered sequentially. (In this case, the boxes are numbered 1 through 8 for identification purposes and for reference to the corresponding overview and detail diagrams.)

hierarchical manner. When the hierarchical method of numbering is used each box should have an identification number of the form $x.y[.z]...$ which corresponds in number and in position to the location of that box in the hierarchy diagram. This technique is shown in Figure 7.4. Each separate number in the identification number, excluding zeros, corresponds to a level in the hierarchy diagram, so boxes numbered 4.1.1 and 4.1.2 are subfunctions of box numbered 4.1 and boxes numbered 3.1, 3.2 and 3.3 are subfunctions of box numbered 3.0.

With the hierarchical numbering scheme, additions can be made without requiring that boxes be renumbered. As shown by the dashed-line boxes in Figure 7.4, additions can be made conveniently and quickly, at any level, as long as the order of steps in a function does not have to be permuted.

The hierarchical numbering scheme also facilitates establishing a correspondence between a box in a hierarchy diagram and other descriptive methods, such as a decision table, a flow chart, or a form layout. Other charts can be given the same number as the corresponding box in the hierarchy diagram with an alphabetic character as a suffix. For example, flow chart numbered 4.1.3A would correspond to box numbered 4.1.3 in the hierarchy diagram. This convention is demonstrated in Figure 7.5.

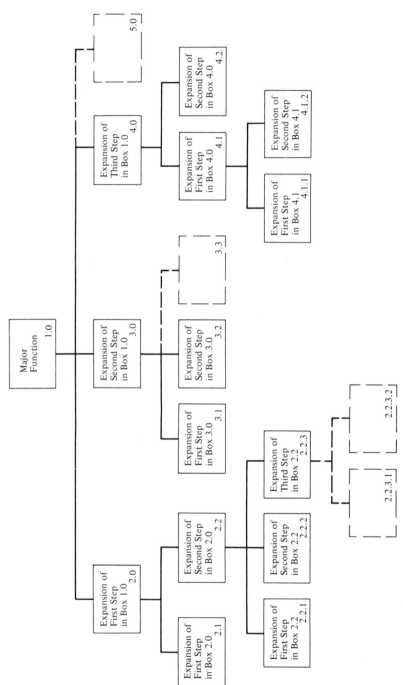

Figure 7.4 In complex hierarchy diagrams or diagrams for which changes are expected, boxes should be numbered in a hierarchical manner to facilitate additions without disturbing the numbering scheme.

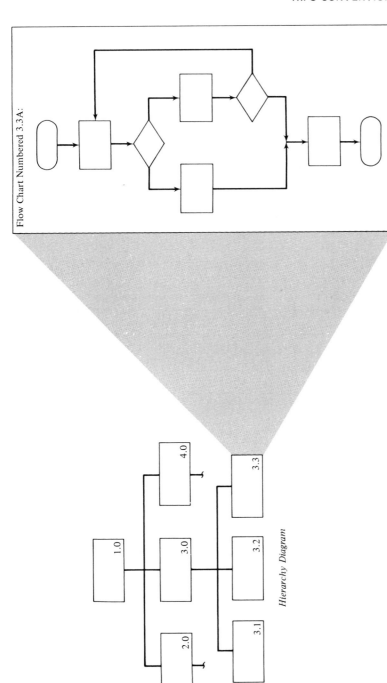

Flow Chart Numbered 3.3A:

Flow Chart

Hierarchy Diagram

Figure 7.5 The hierarchical numbering scheme can be used to establish a correspondence between a box in the hierarchy diagram and another descriptive method, such as a flow chart, by suffixing the box number with an alphabetic character.

A final consideration is the use of the dashed-line boxes for denoting functions performed by another system or functions that have been identified but not yet included in the HIPO package. The choice of either option would be indicated in the legend.

Logical Grouping

Certain functions are used at many points in a system or program. In computer-oriented systems, a logical function of this type might be a utility routine or subroutine that is included only once in the system and called from several places. While logical grouping of this kind implies structure, it is not structure or implementation since objects are treated solely as functions. In noncomputer systems, a logical grouping might correspond to a functional staff that performs a function for an entire organization, such as arrange travel or develop graphic arts material.

If a logical function were included in the hierarchy diagram at each place that it is used, the hierarchy diagram would be unnecessarily complicated and would not accurately represent the system or program. With logical grouping, the function is included only once in the hierarchy diagram and is identified by a shaded corner in its uppermost box, as shown in Figure 7.6.

In the hierarchy diagram, each occurrence of the function is re-

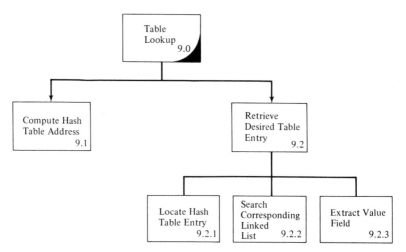

Figure 7.6 A logical function is identified by a shaded corner in the box describing the function.

moved and the corresponding step in the overview or detail diagram is replaced by a reference to an internal routine. As demonstrated in Figure 7.7, the logical function is then placed at the second level in the hierarchy diagram.

It should be emphasized that there is no reference to the logical function in the hierarchy diagram; that is why it is identified by a shaded corner. Actual references to the logical function are made in the overview and detail diagrams.

Number of Levels in a Hierarchy Diagram

While there is no standard for the recommended number of levels in a good hierarchy diagram, the actual number can be determined by practical considerations. A person can absorb only a limited amount of information at a single glance and this normally corresponds to approximately five levels organized somewhat as follows:

1. The uppermost box in the diagram representing the complete system or program.
2. Two levels in the hierarchy diagram that correspond to overview diagrams.
3. Two levels in the hierarchy diagram that correspond to lower-level overview diagrams or detail diagrams.

In general, a hierarchy of hierarchy diagrams should be used if more than five levels are required.

Legend

The legend is optional in a HIPO package but is important enough to be required in most applications of the HIPO technique. A comprehensive legend is given as Figure 7.8

Description Section

No conventions exist for the optional description section of the visual table of contents. The objective of the description section is to provide more information about a particular function than can be obtained from the hierarchy diagram. Since the amount of information that can be placed in a box in the hierarchy diagram is limited practically to a name or a single descriptive phrase, one or two descriptive sentences in the description section would ordinarily be

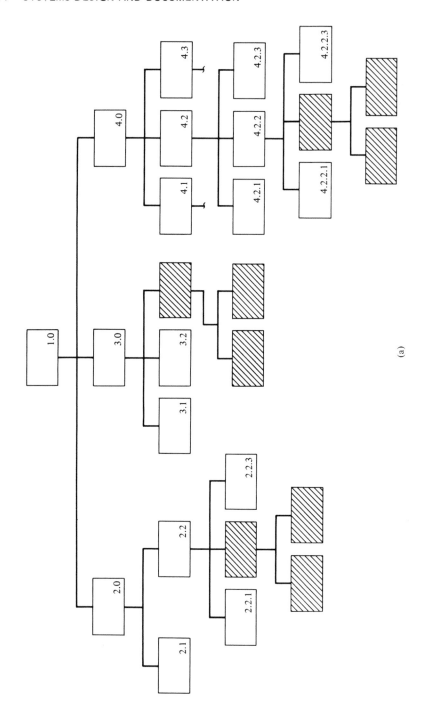

(a)

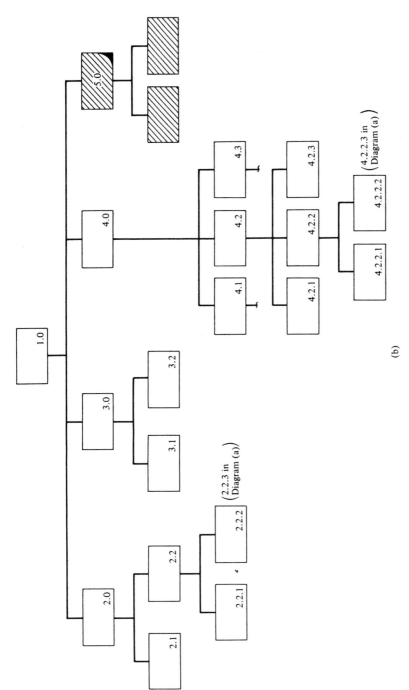

(b)

Figure 7.7   Occurrences of a function that is used at several places in a system or program can be grouped logically to eliminate unnecessary complication in the hierarchy diagram.   (a) Hierarchy diagram showing a logical function (shaded) that is used at several places in a system or program.   (b) Hierarchy diagram showing a logical grouping of functions.

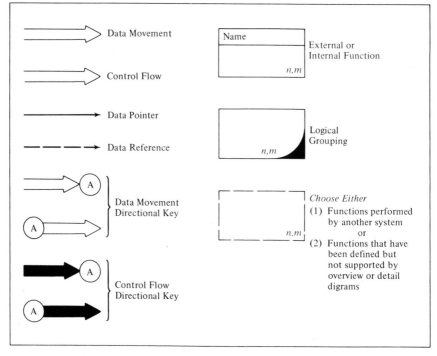

Figure 7.8   Comprehensive legend (for reference purposes).

appropriate. One suggestion is in order here. Normally, the name or phrase in a box in the hierarchy diagram is not repeated in the corresponding entry in the description section because it is redundant.

INPUT AND OUTPUT ENTRIES

In spite of the importance of input and output in the world of computers and data processing, HIPO is one of only a few descriptive techniques that are input and output oriented. There is probably a good reason why input and output are generally neglected, and few people would debate that the reason centers around the fact that describing input and output structure is a messy and cumbersome task while describing the processing aspects of computer utilization is reasonably well defined. As a result of the situation, it is recognized that there should be a considerable amount of leeway as far as input and output representation is concerned. This section gives only a minimum set of operational conventions. A prospective user

Label

Figure 7.9   The general forms of a data entry.

of the HIPO technique can complete his set of conventions personally using the concepts given here as a basis.

Data Entries

A data entry can be represented by a box or by a special symbol representing a particular device or medium. The general form of a data entry is given in Figure 7.9; it can be used to represent input or output entries of any type. (In data processing, an entry may take the form of a file, record, field, storage area, or register.) The *label* (i.e., the *name* of the entry) identifies the entry as it is referenced in the process box, and the *descriptive information* supplements the label for cases in which subunits of data are referenced. Several examples of data entries are given in Figure 7.10. A general rule of thumb is that only subunits of data used in the process block should be indicated in an input or output entry and the relative order of subunits in a data entry is not significant.

Special Symbols

When it is necessary to associate a data entry with a specific device type or medium, the standard flow chart symbols, given in Figure

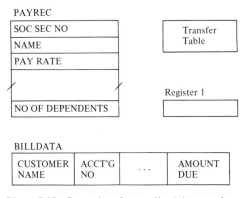

Figure 7.10   Examples of generalized data entries.

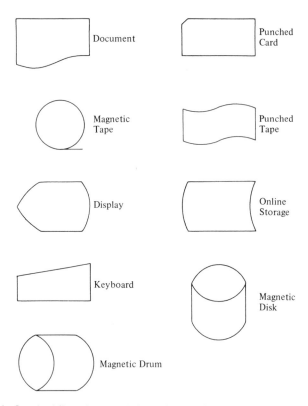

Figure 7.11   Standard flow chart symbols can be used for specific device types or media.

7.11, can be used. In this case, the name of the data entry is normally placed inside of the flow chart symbol.

Repeated Data Movement

Repeated data movement refers to the case where the same input entry is used in more than one step in the process block or an output entry is created or updated by more than one step in the process block. Repeated data movement can be denoted in several ways; the particular choice of method is dependent upon the application and the diagramming conventions established by the design, implementation, or documentation group. The choices are:

1. Draw a single data movement arrow from the input data entry to the steps, which must be consecutive, in the process block and are enclosed in a box.

1a. Draw a single data movement arrow from the steps, which must be consecutive, in the process block and are enclosed in a box to the output data entry.

(Choices 1 and 1a are demonstrated in Figure 7.12.)

2. Draw a multiple arrow with one tail and several heads from the input data entry to the steps in the process block.

2a. Draw a multiple arrow with several tails and one head from the steps in the process block to the output data entry.

(Choices 2 and 2a are demonstrated in Figure 7.13.)

3. Use a directional key from the data entry in the input block with an input directional key to each of the steps in the process block that use that entry.

3a. Use an output directional key from each step in the process block that generates a particular entry and a directional key to the data entry in the output block.

(Choices 3 and 3a are demonstrated in Figure 7.14.)

4. Insert a separate occurrence of the data entry in the input block with a data movement arrow to the step in the process block for each time that it is used.

4a. Insert a separate occurrence of the data entry in the output block with a data movement arrow from each step in the process block that creates or updates it.

(Choices 4 and 4a are demonstrated in Figure 7.15.) In general, however, the use of multiple occurrences of the same data entries for representing repeated data movement should be discouraged unless a means is available for indicating that the multiplicity of the same entry exists.

The various techniques for representing repeated data movement can be used in combination, and arrows may cross over each other provided that the visual impression is unambiguous. For example, Figure 7.16 communicates the same information as Figure 7.15, except that crossed arrows are used.

Updated Data Entries

When a data entry serves as input to a step in the process block and is updated in that step or by a subsequent step in the same process

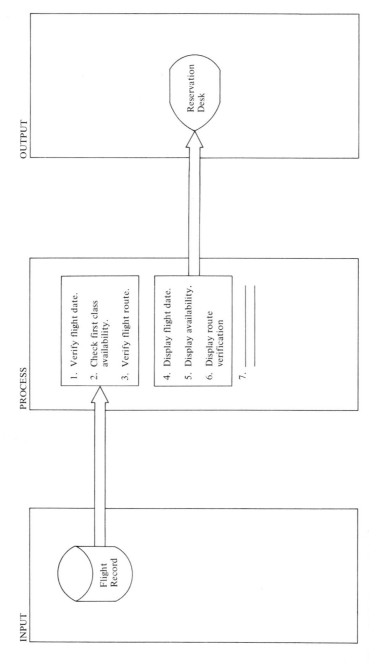

Figure 7.12 Repeated data movement can be represented by enclosing the steps in the process block in a box and by using a single data movement arrow.

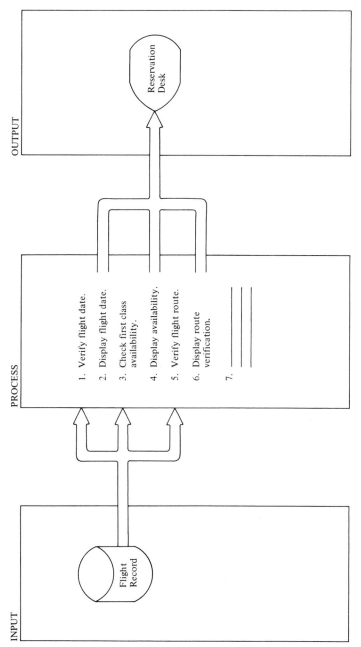

Figure 7.13   Repeated data movement can be represented by using a multiple arrow.

INPUT

Flight
Record

PROCESS

1. Verify flight date.

2. Display flight date.

3. Check first class
   availability.

4. Display availability.

5. Verify flight route.

6. Display route
   verification.

7.

OUTPUT

Reservation
Desk

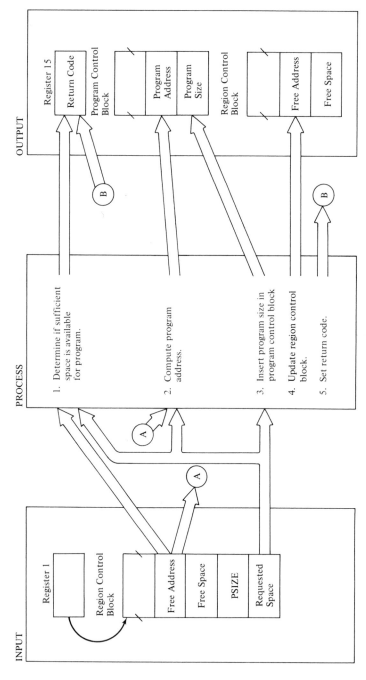

Figure 7.14   Repeated movement can be represented by directional keys.

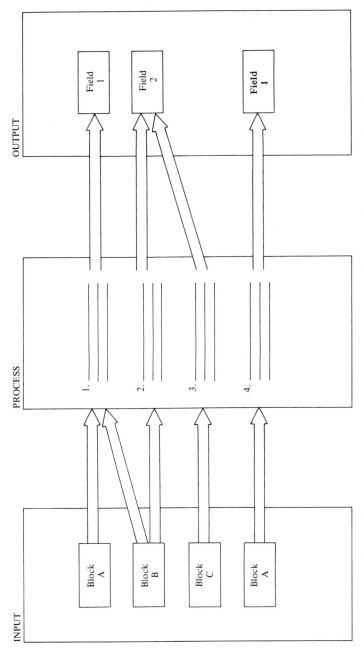

Figure 7.15   The use of multiple occurrences of the same data entry is another means of representing multiple data movement.

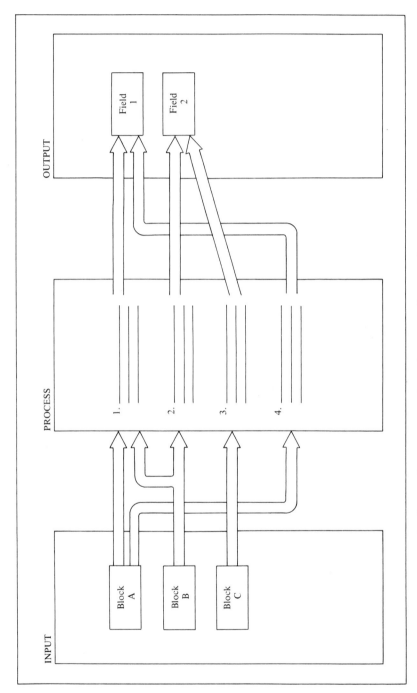

Figure 7.16 The use of a crossed arrow is another means of representing repeated data movement.

block, the method of representation can easily lead to confusion, especially for the occasional user of the HIPO technique. A general rule to be applied to this and similar cases is that, *the input block should be used exclusively for input data entries.* The confusing and preferred forms of an updated data entry are demonstrated in Figure 7.17. The confusion arises when an updated data entry is used as input to a subsequent step in the process and it is necessary to specify whether the original or the updated version is to be used.

Created vs. Updated Data Entries

Most examples given in this and preceding chapters demonstrate data entries that serve as input or output—but not both. Thus, a single occurrence of a data entry in the output block is implicitly represented as being *created* by one or more steps in the process block. On the other hand, a data entry in the output block is represented as being *updated* when it also appears in the input block as input to a step in the process block. In the case of an updated data entry, however, the input step must precede the output. Figure 7.18 depicts an input/output sequence that does not make sense, unless two versions of the JCT data entry are used. The task of editing HIPO diagrams is covered in a subsequent section.

Output Data Entries Used as Input

An output data entry that is created or updated in one or more steps in the process block and is used as input to a later step in the process block is represented in the output block, as shown in Figure 7.19, which demonstrates the case of a created output data entry. Thus, an output data entry serves also as an input entry that is contained in the output block. This leads to another useful rule: An output block may be used to represent input data entries, in addition to output data entries, but only if they have been generated by a step in the process block. The use of an updated output data entry that is used as input to a later step in the process block is shown in Figure 7.20. It is clear from the HIPO diagram in Figure 7.20 that the updated version of the master file is used as input to steps numbered 2 and 3 of the process block.

Figure 7.20 also demonstrates the use of a double-headed arrow to

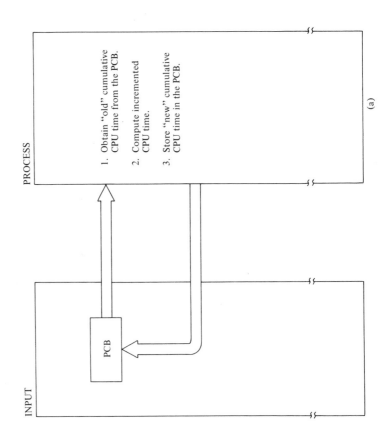

(a)

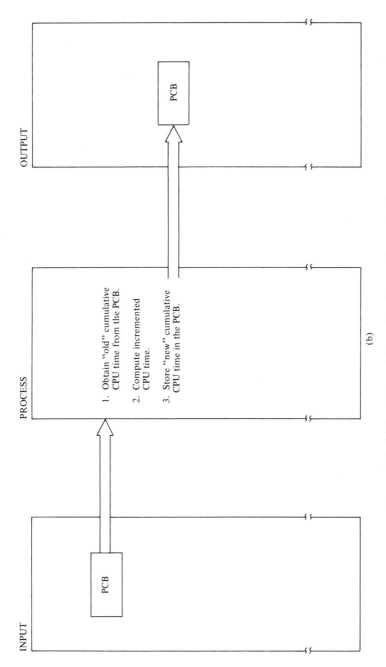

Figure 7.17 (a) Confusing and (b) preferred forms of an updated entry.

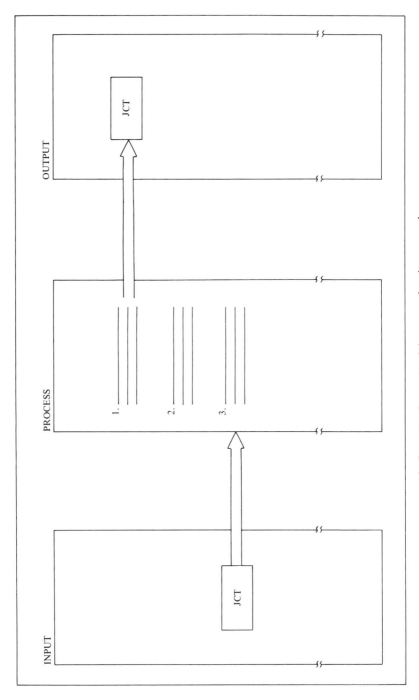

Figure 7.18 Example of an updated data entry that does not make sense.

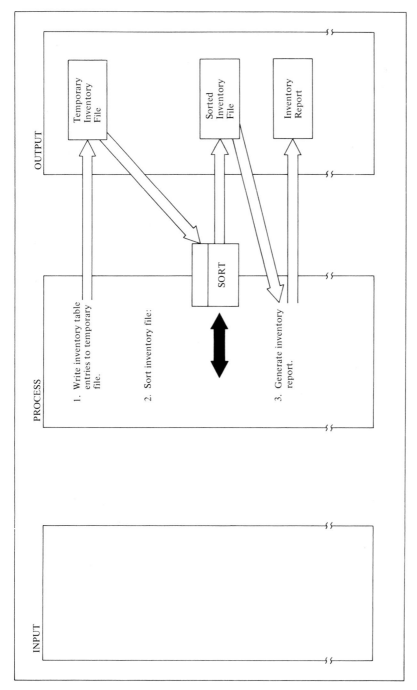

Figure 7.19   Example of created output entries that are used as input to later steps in the process block.

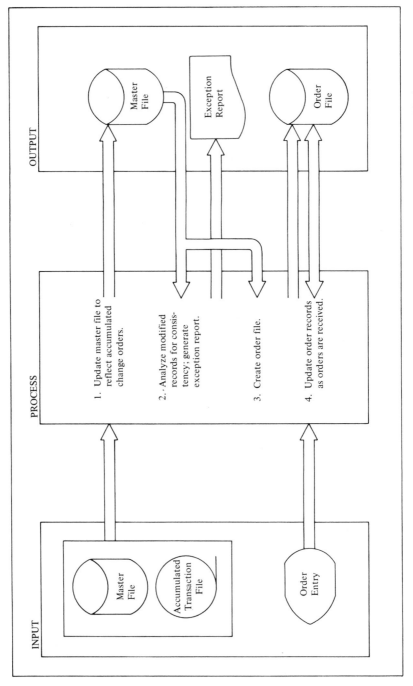

Figure 7.20   Example of updated output data entries that are used as input to later steps in the process block.

denote data movement when an output data entry is used as both output and input to the same step in the process block.

Repeated Data Movement with Update

When a case of repeated data movement is combined with an update step in the process block, the manner of representation determines how the diagram is interpreted. Figure 7.21 demonstrates a typical case. Repeated data input using the original input should emanate from the input block; repeated data input that uses the updated version of the data entry should, in all cases, emanate from the output block. In the upper diagram of Figure 7.21, for example, it is clearly evident that the input to step 3 is the updated version of LRK, and this effect is achieved through the visual impression that is created by the diagram. In the lower diagram of Figure 7.21, it is clearly evident that the original version of LRK is used as input to steps 1 and 3, and that the updated version of LRK is used as input to step 4.

Combined Input

A phenomenon that occurs frequently in systems work involves input that is multiplexed. In data processing systems, an example of multiplexing is the case where a record is read from one file, such as a transaction file, and then the next record is read from a second file, such as a master file. The process is repeated throughout the processing cycle as is commonly the case for merging, collating, and sorting operations. In non-data processing systems, multiplexing might occur, for example, when one expert's opinion is sampled, then another expert's opinion is sampled, etc., until a consensus of opinion or a stalemate is achieved.

Multiplexed input is referred to as *combined input* and is represented in two ways:

1. When the input data entries are adjacent to each other, they can be enclosed in a box and a single data movement arrow can be used.
2. The data movement arrows from the data entries can be joined before they enter the process block.

The methods are demonstrated in Figure 7.22. The practice of join-

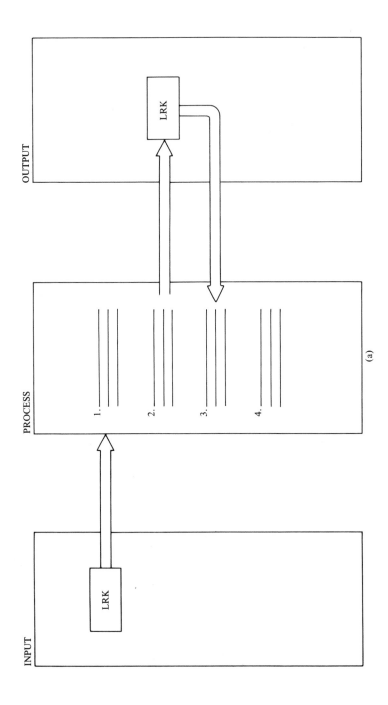

(a)

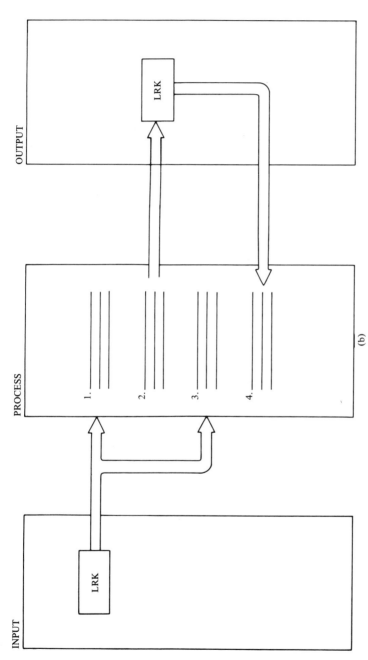

Figure 7.21 The manner in which a repeated data entry is represented determines how it is interpreted. (a) Updated data entry used in step three. (b) Original data entry used in step three; updated data entry used in step four.

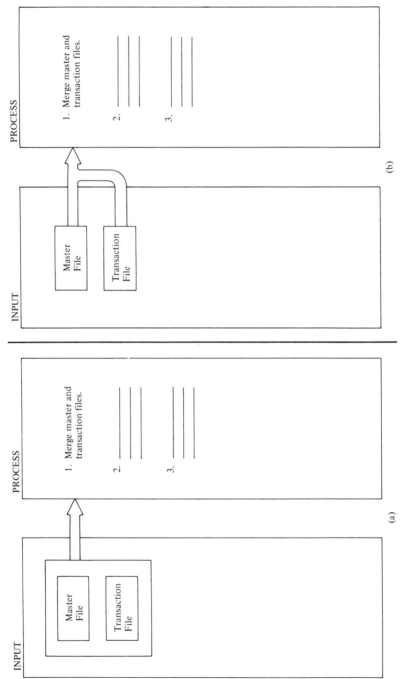

Figure 7.22 Two methods of representing combined input. (a) Data entries can be enclosed in a box. (b) Data movement arrows can be joined.

ing data movement arrows is particularly useful when the data entries are not adjacent and data crossing arrows can be used.

Repeated and Combined Data Reference

Although crossing arrows should be avoided whenever possible, effective graphics can eliminate ambiguities when data movement arrows are used by drawing an arrow so that it gives the visual impression of being above or below another arrow.

An ambiguous use of data reference arrows is demonstrated in Figure 7.23; difficulty arises because it is not clear whether repeated input or combined input is meant and to which junction the vertical arrow should be connected. The situation can be resolved by placing an arrowhead at the intended junction and by using multiple arrows to increase graphic fidelity.   Figure 7.24 depicts an unambiguous version of Figure 7.23 depicting combined input, and Figure 7.25 depicts an unambiguous version of the same diagram demonstrating repeated input.

Input and Output Graphics

Consistency is an important ingredient of effective HIPO documentation, and in most cases, the fact that a diagramming convention is consistently applied is more significant than the convention itself. For input, a data movement arrow should begin at the right-hand edge of the data entry and terminate at the number of the step in the process block that uses it.   Directional keys and arrow crossings should be placed in the space between the input and process blocks. A data movement arrow should be shown graphically as though it were placed *above* the right-hand edge of the input block. Input and output graphics are summarized in Figure 7.26.

For output, a data movement arrow should begin at the right-hand edge of the text for the step in the process block and terminate at the left-hand edge of the data entry symbol in the output block. As with input, crossings and keys should be placed between the process and output blocks, and data movement arrows should be graphically raised above the edges of the process and output blocks. As shown in Figure 7.26, the beginning of the output data movement arrows should be aligned near the right-hand edge of the process block.

The only exception to the above conventions exists for overview

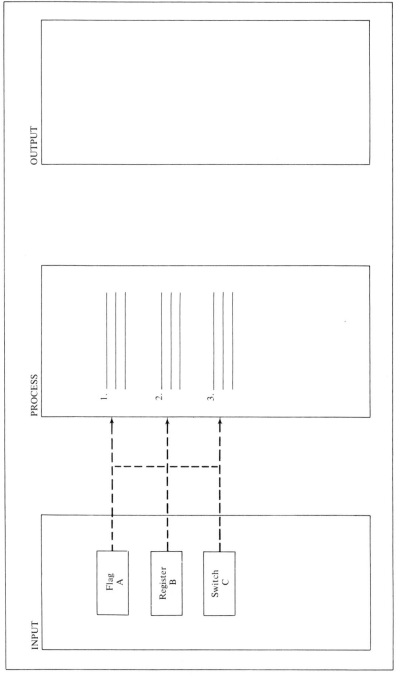

Figure 7.23 An ambiguous use of data reference arrows. It is not evident whether repeated or combined input is intended and which junction should be used.

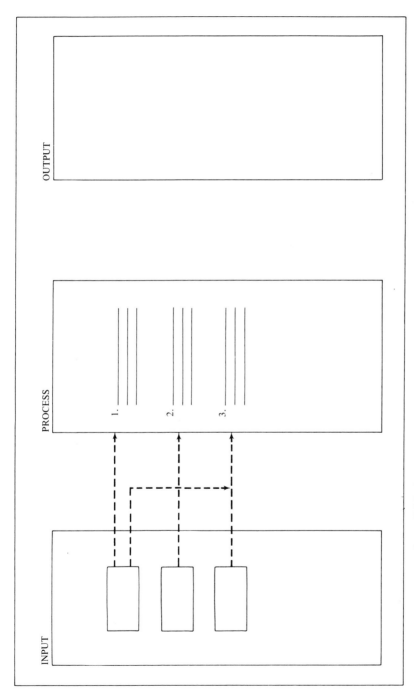

Figure 7.24 An unambiguous version of Figure 7.23 showing combined data reference.

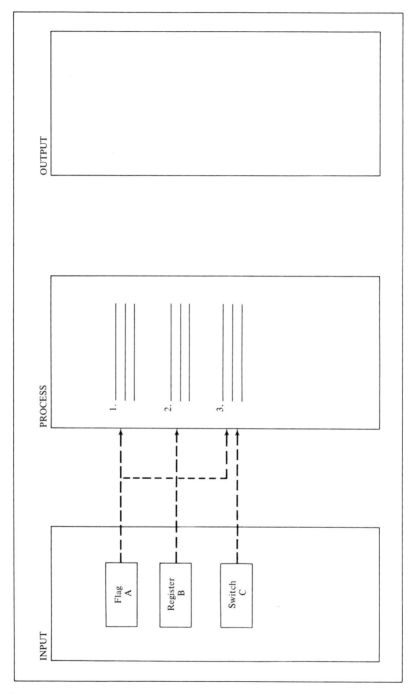

Figure 7.25   An alternate version of Figure 7.23 showing repeated data reference.

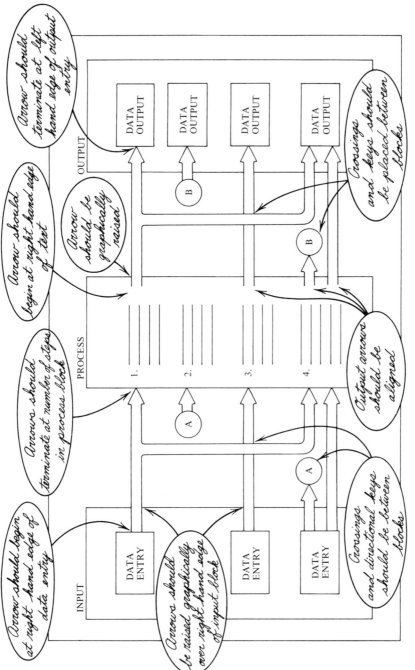

Figure 7.26 Input and output graphics.

diagrams in which there is a single arrow from the input block to the process block and a single arrow from the process block to the output block. In this case, the input arrow should begin at the right-hand edge of the input block and terminate at the left-hand edge of the process block; the output arrow should begin at the right-hand edge of the process block and terminate at the left-hand edge of the output block.

PROCESS BLOCK

The purpose of the process block is to delineate the steps that comprise a functional component of a system. Within a function, each step represents a subfunction, and the method of representation can be continued for as many levels as is necessary to describe a system. The exact composition of the process block is dependent upon three factors:

1. The type of HIPO package.
2. The level in the hierarchy diagram.
3. The type of system being described.

Thus, a certain amount of variation can be expected to occur between process blocks for different types of HIPO packages, between process blocks for different levels in the same package, and between HIPO packages for different systems. The following conventions can be used to reduce the variations between HIPO packages and enable systems concepts to be more readily understood.

Steps in the Process Block

Each step in the process block should be assigned a number, and the various steps that comprise the block should be numbered consecutively starting with the number 1. The numbers may be placed in small circles or boxes, representing keys, or be simply followed by a period. The key is used to establish a correspondence between a step in the process block and an entry in the extended description.

Except at the lowest level in the hierarchy diagram, each step in the process block is described further in a lower-level diagram. The existence of a lower-level diagram is indicated in one of two principal ways:

1. By enclosing the step in a box and by placing the identification

number of the corresponding lower-level diagram in the lower right-hand corner of the box. This alternative is demonstrated in Figure 7.27 and is the preferred method.

2. By placing the identification number of the lower-level diagram in the corresponding entry in the extended description. In general, this alternative is not preferred because it necessitates the use of the extended description for higher-level diagrams.

The number of steps that should be placed in the process block is related, conceptually, to the number of levels in the hierarchy diagram. From five to seven steps is a practical limitation. The actual number is dependent upon the amount of information that can be absorbed in a short period of time and on the physical size of the diagram. If more than five to seven steps are required, then the various functions should be subdivided in a more judicious manner.

Imperative Verbs

Each step in a process block should consist of a *brief* statement of the function that is performed. If it is necessary to provide more information to the reader, then an extended description should be used.

One successful approach to developing a brief statement of a function is to begin the statement with an imperative statement, such as CREATE, EDIT, LOAD, READ, or TEST. A representative list of imperative verbs is given in Table 7.1

Control within the Process Block

In higher-level diagrams, the steps in the process block are normally executed in the order in which they are listed. This is particularly true in light of the fact that imperative verbs should be used, as indicated above, and that they represent functions. In lower-level diagrams, however, it is frequently impossible to eliminate conditional and control operations completely—especially when a computer program is being documented. Therefore, as demonstrated in Figure 7.28, a control arrow with directional keys can be used to denote the conditional or unconditional transfer of control from one step to another step.

When a control arrow is used with a directional key, the key contains the number of the step in the process block to which the arrow

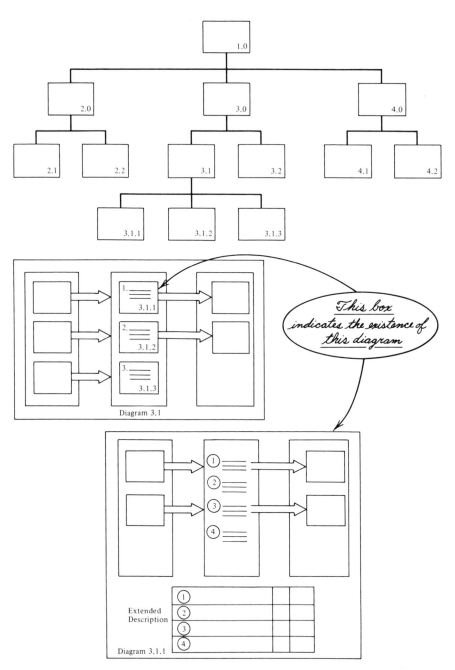

Figure 7.27 The presence of a lower-level diagram is indicated by enclosing a step of the process block in a box and by placing the identification number of the lower-level diagram in the lower right-hand corner of the box.

TABLE 7.1   REPRESENTATIVE LIST OF IMPERATIVE VERBS FOR USE
IN THE PROCESS BLOCK. (Reprinted with permission from:
HIPO—A Design Aid and Documentation Technique, IBM Corporation, Form GC20-1851, p. 63.)

accept	delete	get	perform	select
add	dequeue	handle	place	set
allocate	detach	identify	position	specify
alter	determine	increment	post	start
analyze	display	initialize	process	stop
assign	do until	insert	provide	store
begin	do while	issue	purge	supply
build	edit	locate	put	suspend
calculate	encode	link	queue	switch
check	enqueue	load	read	terminate
clear	enter	look up	record	test
close	establish	maintain	reinstate	transfer
complete	examine	make	release	translate
construct	execute	merge	resolve	update
control	exit	modify	restore	use
convert	extract	monitor	return	validate
copy	find	move	scan	verify
create	fix	obtain	schedule	write
decrement	format	open	search	

directs control. In Figure 7.28, for example, the output control arrow from step 3 denotes that control should continue with step 5. Similarly, the output control arrow from step 4 corresponds to the input control arrow attached to step 1.

In special cases, an offpage control arrow can be used to transfer control to another system, program, or function. The form of an offpage control arrow is given in Figure 7.29. However, the use of offpage control arrows represents a nonstandard application of the HIPO technique, since the systems participating in the intersystem coordination could probably have been combined in the first place.

Control Into and Out of the Process Block

It was mentioned earlier that the hierarchy diagram should be read from left to right, at any level in the diagram. Thus, for example, the reader would normally go from diagram 3.1.1 to 3.1.2, and so forth. When a hierarchy diagram contains a uniform number of levels, no other control information is necessary. However, more explicit control information is necessary when the number of levels

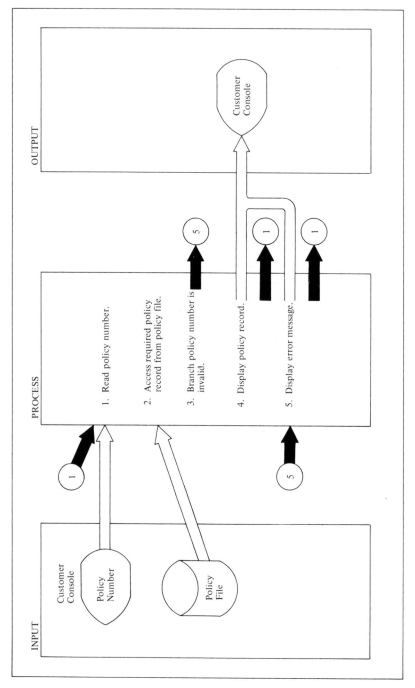

Figure 7.28 The control arrow with directional keys can be used to indicate control operations in the process block.

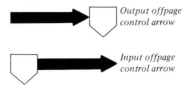

*Output offpage
control arrow*

*Input offpage
control arrow*

Figure 7.29   The form of an offpage control arrow. *Name* refers to the name of the system, program, or function, and *ID* is the identification number of the HIPO diagram in that HIPO package.

is not uniform or the functions that comprise the system are organized in a hierarchical manner. The former case is referred to as sequential control. The latter case is known as hierarchical control.

With *sequential control,* each overview or detail diagram in the HIPO package is labeled with the predecessor and with the successor diagram in the system description.   In Figure 7.30, for example, control flows from diagram 3.2.1 to 3.2.2 to 3.2.3 and that fact is indicated by the "from" and "to" control arrows that lead into and out of the process block.   The arrows may be curved, as shown in Figure 7.30, or straight, as shown in Figure 7.31.   The choice of a particular type of arrow is dependent upon graphical considerations, since both types of arrows are logically equivalent.   The practice of labeling the "from" and "to" arrows allows the reader to go from one diagram to another without having to reference the hierarchy diagram in the visual table of contents.

With *hierarchical control,* the hierarchy diagram may be read from top to bottom, as might be the case with structured programming or top-down development. In this case, for example, diagram 3.0 would logically "call" diagrams 3.1, 3.2, 3.3, etc. and then diagrams 3.1, 3.2, and 3.3 would normally return to diagram 3.0.   Hierarchical control is demonstrated in Figure 7.32, in which the calling block is denoted by the "from" control arrow.   The "return" arrow is not labeled since control is always returned to the calling block. As with sequential control, curved or straight control arrows may be used with hierarchical control.

Sequential and hierarchical control are both used in effective HIPO diagramming. Sequential control is the preferred method and is used for describing all system functions—with one exception. Functions described by logical grouping would require hierarchical

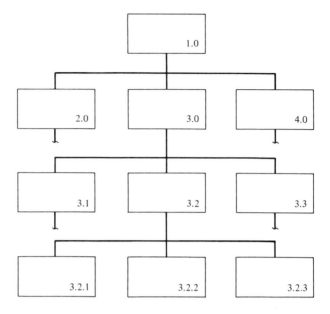

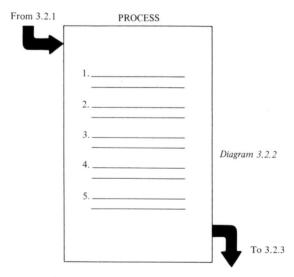

Figure 7.30   Sequential control of flow in and out of the process block. The "from" and "to" blocks are denoted by curved control arrows. (In this case, control goes from diagram 3.2.1 to 3.2.2 to 3.2.3.)

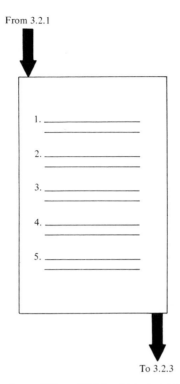

Figure 7.31   An alternate form of Figure 7.30 in which straight control arrows are used.

control arrows since the corresponding function would be referenced at several points in the system.

Internal References

A function that is part of the system (or program) being described
and can be referenced from several places in the system (or program)
is described through the use of the logical grouping concept.

A reference to a function contained in a system or program is
known as an *internal reference,* which is represented by the "subroutine" symbols shown in Figure 7.33.   A double-headed control
arrow is used when control is returned to the calling function, and
the single-headed control arrow is used when control is not returned
to the calling function.

An example of an internal reference is shown in Figure 7.34.   An

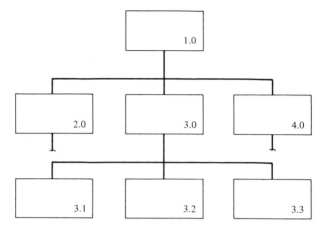

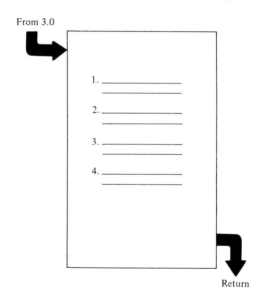

Figure 7.32 Hierarchical control of flow into and out of the process block. The calling block is denoted by the "from" control arrow. A return is made to the calling block. (In this case, diagram 3.0 calls diagrams 3.1, 3.2, and 3.3.)

internal reference is denoted by the fact that the subroutine block is enclosed completely in the process block. The identification number of the HIPO diagram describing the internal function is placed in the lower right-hand corner of the internal reference symbol. Alter-

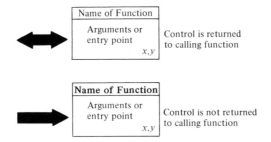

Figure 7.33   Symbols used for internal and external references.

nately, the identification number of the internally referenced function may be placed in the extended description.

External References

An *external reference* is a reference to a function that is not logically contained in the system being described by the HIPO package. An external reference is identical to an internal reference except for the

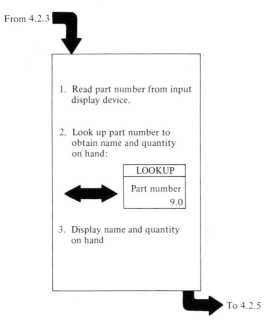

Figure 7.34   An example of an internal reference.   The "subroutine" symbol is enclosed *within* the process block.

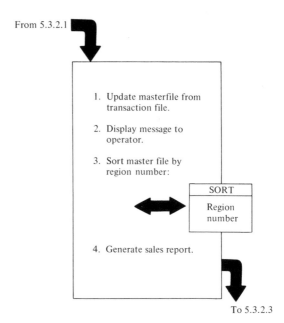

From 5.3.2.1

1. Update masterfile from transaction file.

2. Display message to operator.

3. Sort master file by region number:

SORT

Region number

4. Generate sales report.

To 5.3.2.3

Figure 7.35   An example of an external reference. The "subroutine" symbol is placed *on* the right-hand edge of the process block.

fact that the external reference symbol is not enclosed in the process block; it is placed on the right-hand edge of the process block as demonstrated in Figure 7.35. If the external reference is described by a HIPO diagram or a HIPO package, it should be noted in the reference symbol as indicated above.

The difference between internal and external references, as far as HIPO diagramming is concerned, is graphical and is intended to indicate the type of reference at a glance.

EDITING OF HIPO DIAGRAMS

For new systems, HIPO diagrams are prepared initially by the design and implementation groups and edited by the documentation group. For existing systems, the documentation group may prepare and edit the HIPO diagrams. In either case, it is usually the role of the documentation group to polish a HIPO package so it is an effective means of communication.

In editing a HIPO package, the documentation group should consider five major points:

1. Organization.

2. Level of detail.
3. Transitions.
4. Consistency.
5. Technical accuracy.

In fact, the five areas may form a checklist for review and official sign-offs.

Organization refers to the package as a whole. Each diagram should play a role in the communication process and the functional structure of the system, and the documentation as well, should reflect good planning and logical organization.

The *level of detail* in a HIPO package must be sufficient to describe the system in an unambiguous manner and to specify needed information for user, maintenance, and training groups. At the opposite extreme, the HIPO package should not contain excessive detail so that it is impossible to determine the objective of the system.

The *transition* between the HIPO diagrams, both horizontally and vertically, should be clearly evident. Through the effective use of identification numbers, keys, and control arrows, the reader should be able to isolate a needed description of a function without having to search through the entire HIPO package.

HIPO diagrams should be *consistent* in form and content. The level of detail should be uniform throughout the package and the HIPO conventions and graphic symbols should be consistently applied.

A HIPO package should be *technically accurate.* Needed information should not be missing and all diagrams should be meaningful at a given level of detail. The use of graphic symbols should not be carelessly applied so as to confuse the reader. In fact, a final HIPO package should be reviewed by design and implementation groups to insure that it is technically accurate.

Clearly, the five major areas of HIPO editing are related. However, overall adherence to firm standards in *each* of these areas will help to insure that effective documentation is produced.

REFERENCES

HIPO—A Design Aid and Documentation Technique, White Plains, New York, IBM Corporation, 1974, Form GC20-1851.

HIPO: Design Aid and Documentation Tool, Poughkeepsie, New York, IBM Corporation, 1973, Form SR20-9413.

INDEX

INDEX